AF632341

India in Canadian Imagination

A Literary Response

India in Canadian Imagination

A Literary Response

edited by

R.K. Dhawan
D.K. Pabby
S.S. Sharma

PRESTIGE

Published by
Prestige Books
3/28, East Patel Nagar
New Delhi 110 008

ISBN: 81-7551-138-9

Copyright Editor, 2003

All rights reserved. No part of this book may be reproduced or utilized in any form or by any means, electronic or mechanical, including photocopy, microfilm, microfiche, recording, e-mail, web publication, or any information storage and retrieval system, without the written permission of the copyright owner.

Printed at Chaman Offset Press, New Delhi 110 002

Contents

India in Canadian Imagination

R.K. DHAWAN
S.B.S. College, University of Delhi

In the history of mankind, we find that man has always been going out of the bounds of the immediate social group he belonged to, and have social, economic or literary exchange with people belonging to other communities. This is because there is a marked distinction between different ethnic entities; human nature is curious to know and explore the world beyond the immediate reality. It is true therefore that human civilization has been enriched by the cross-fertilization of ideas. It is virtually human desire that motivates us to know more about others specifically to form ideas or conceive images about other nations and peoples.

It is well known that the imprint of Indian thought or the image of India in the West covers a wide range of subjects. Writers in Europe and America, as is evident in their literary works, have perceived a diverse and highly complex picture of India. Many scholars and writers have endeavoured to explore the inexhaustible heritage of Indian thought, life and society. India, to the Westerners, has been traditionally a land of culture, grandeur and dignity. To some, it is a land of miracles, a land where Sathya Sai Baba and other yogis can do wonders, a land known for yoga and spiritualism, a land where strange things happen and a place where everything is fascinating and exotic.

Malraux, for example, had a profound fascination for India. To him, India belongs to the ancient Orient of the soul because it is less westernized and spreads wide the 'nocturnal wings' of man. Malraux visited India five times between 1929 to 1974. He found a great solace and comfort in Indian culture and civilization. For the Europeans distressed by the horrors of the world wars and by the disintegration of western values, the serenity of the Himalayas and the wisdom of great thinkers of India constituted a great source of inspiration.

Interestingly, there is another set of people, rather a vast number in the West, who regard India as a backward country where orthodoxy, corruption and bribery is a way of life. These are floating images based on isolated and fragmentary glimpses of life and society as it exists in India today. India is known for its unity in diversity. The people of this country, despite their glorious past, had been enslaved for centuries. There is a marked change in the India of today from the milieu of the pre-Independence period.

India has been depicted in the literatures being written in the West. It must however be noted that it is mainly the writers of Indian diasporas who have portrayed the country of their origin or that of their forefathers. This is true of the literature being produced in Canada. The white Canadians like Sara Duncan and a host of other writers have given expression to their idea of India in various literary forms, but the literature produced by diasporic writers is both substantial and worth consideration.

Expatriation as a literary phenomenon assumes intense importance in the twenty-first century owing to large-scale emigration. Indians, Pakistanis, Bangladeshis and Sri Lankans, settled abroad, have made a substantial contribution. South Asian diasporic writing or the diasporic literature of the Indian subcontinent shares a common diasporic consciousness and a structural and thematic framework which needs to be examined at length. An overwhelming majority of South Asian writers is 'Indian' in the sense that they could trace their routes to the India of the pre-Partition 1947 when Pakistan and Bangla Desh were very much its part. Amazingly, the South Asian diaspora currently exceeds eleven million people. It is widely spread across the world and is varied in character. People of the South Asian origin now reside in over seventy countries, across all the continents of the world. While initially the South Asian population migrated in search of work, once they were in new lands, this diaspora contributed to different walks of life in those countries, including intellectual and literary scene. No wonder, several of the South Asian diasporic writers have received international recognition. These writers are known for introducing new themes and diverse techniques in their works. Expatriate/diasporic writers in the recent years have created a unique form of literature which indulges in nostalgia, yet at the same time forging identity with new place and people. Diaspora is thus no more a painful experience in alienation or marginalization, for the individual writers of the South Asian diaspora, in their writings, have made a rich and varied response to the experience of migration. The sense of homelessness and nostalgia for the lost haven is surely one of the most important themes in literature. On the one hand, they regret the loss of land they left behind, mythologizing it through memory, nostalgia and imagination. On the other hand, they make expatriation a positive act of distancing and achieving a true perspective in life and situation. In this respect, diaspora achieves the unintended purpose of celebrating marginality and embracing virtually multiculturalism and diversity. This is evident from the fast growing South Asian diasporic writing. Some of the significant writers are: in England: V.S. Naipaul, Salman Rushdie, Farrukh Dhondy, Suniti Namjoshi, Leela Dhingra and Meera Syal (India), Hanif Kureishi and Alifquar Ghose (Pakistan); in Canada: Rohinton Mistry, B. Rajan, Uma Parameswaran, Himani Banerjee, Rahul Varma, Rana Bose (India) and Michael Ondaatje (Sri Lanka); in America: Bharati Mukherjee, Jhumpa Lahiri, A.K. Ramanujan, Meena Alexander, Shashi Tharoor, Chitra Banerjee Divakaruni, Geeta Mehta, Ved Mehta (India), Bapsi Sidhwa (Pakistan) and several Sri Lankan writers including Romesh Gunasekara, Shyam Selvadurai, Daya de Silva and Sarika Thiranagama; in Australia: Mena Abdullah, Bem le Hunte, Suneeta Peres de Costa (India), Adib Khan (Bangla Desh), Chitra Fernando, Yasmine Gooneratne, Chandani Lokuge (Sri Lanka)

Immigrant writing is important, for emigration has been seen as an escape from the communal, economic and political chaos which prevailed in the native land. Entering the much sought-after life in the West, what does the immigrant writer find? How does India figure in his imagination? It is sometimes a love-hate relationship. For immigrants like Uma Parameswaran, Bharati Mukherjee, Rohinton Mistry, Anita Rau Badami and Shauna Singh Baldwin, confrontation with another society starts the process of deconstructing and restructuring the self.

It is an accepted and acknowledged fact of the literary history of North America in general and Canada in particular that 'Immigrant Writing' or 'Diasporic Writing' is fast emerging as a distinct and well-identifiable category. In the case of Canada, which is otherwise largely inhabited by the immigrants from all over the world, migrated population from Indian subcontinent forms a significant segment. The situation of a 'mosaic' as against 'a melting pot' in the U.S.A. makes Canada a better sought-after destination as compared to America. Canada also occupies a unique position owing to the fact that it is one of those very few countries that have exhibited much courage in officially putting on their statute book A Multicultural Policy and A Multicultural Act. In fact, the Policy and the Act are significant government initiatives aimed at efficient management of their ethno-cultural diversity. Used prescriptively, multiculturalism in Canada encompasses a relatively coherent set of ideas and ideals in defence of 'celebrating diversity' as a positive, central and valued component of the Canadian mosaic. The Policy and the Act have emerged due to five hundred years of continuous immigration to Canada. As a natural consequence of this, preserving of linguistic, cultural and literary heritage has endowed the Canadian society with a vibrancy and richness that several other societies lack. This is a society in which the charter groups, indigenous communities and the immigrant rub shoulders with one another in all walks of life. But no system is perfect in all respects. There are some inter-community and inter-cultural conflicts that the immigrants bring in train from their native homes, cultures and countries. It is this complexity of the multicultural society of Canada that has resulted in growth of a distinct diasporic literature with its own flavour and fragrance. The writers of Indian origin writing largely in English have developed a category of their own which can well be designated as CIDW i.e. Canadian Indian Diasporic Writing. The significant contributors to this category are: Rohinton Mistry, M.G. Vassanji, Rana Bose, Rahul Verma, Suniti Namjoshi, Uma Parameswaran, Lakshmi Gill, Stephen Gill, Anita Rau Badami, Shauna Singh Baldwin, Hiro Boga et al. These creative writers are now recognized in Canada at par with the mainstream writers. They are also given their due in India as there is a lot of India in their creative imagination and their writings present an objective perspective of the Indian society. Some of them are now prescribed in several Indian universities and abroad. Besides being the subject of research in newly-emerging fields such as 'Going back to the Roots,' 'Constructing Communities,' 'Establishing Linkages' etc.

The present collection of essays seeks to analyze the reflection of Indian thought and reality as depicted in Canadian literature. Interestingly, Canada and India are separated not only by thousands of miles but also by different histories, cultures and traditions; in spite of this fact both these countries have many similarities especially in terms of language, polity and multicultural ethos. Despite certain differences and similarities, Canadians seem fascinated by India. It is therefore both interesting and rewarding to evaluate how India figures in Canadian imagination.

Fiction across Worlds: Some Writers of Indian Origin in Canada

M.L. PANDIT
IGNOU, New Delhi

The Commonwealth is a brotherhood of states spread over all the five continents of the world. The nations that form parts of it have much more in common than only the English language. The Commonwealth countries share areas of creative interest that are often missing in other federations based on common geographical, economic or political considerations. The Canadian nation consists of a multiplicity of races and cultures that is rarely encountered outside the Commonwealth. From time to time, through accidents of history, a variety of people of different races, backgrounds and cultures have sought refuge in this country of the English and French speaking peoples. Multiculturalism is an essential aspect of the Canadian scene, and it is reflected in the works of the writers of this land. It should come as no surprise that their imagination leaps across worlds in search of suitable themes and motifs for creative writing.

There is a great variety in the Canadian immigrant experience as recorded in literature. During the last fifty years, many writers of Indian origin, once or twice removed from their first homeland, have gone as immigrants to Canada. One of the foremost among them was Bharati Mukherjee—now in the USA—who could boast of a triple inheritance from her Bengali Indian antecedents to the years spent in an American university and to the subsequent experience of living and teaching in Canada. In works like *Wife* (1976) and *Jasmine* (1990), she provides a realistic account of the pressures facing an Indian woman in a male-dominated North American society. In collaboration with Clark Blaise, her America-born husband, Bharati Mukherjee wrote a dual autobiography, *Days and Nights in Calcutta* (1977). It is an account of a year they spent together in India. She went to revisit a world she had left, to explore a world he had married into. The contrast between the two parts of the book stresses the difference in their points of view. Clark Blaise sees the richness of India and the strangeness of his experience. He faithfully records the events of their journey together, as any other foreign tourist would do. Bharati Mukherjee, on the other hand, with her knowledge of Bengali, hears gossip, pain, pressure and privilege of the people she encounters. The same episodes carry different overtones in the two separate accounts. It is the difference between an outsider's and an insider's view. With the publication of the book back in the West, it highlights the contrast between a native and a foreign writer.

The immigrant writer's contribution is best illustrated by a short story, which comes at the end of *The Middleman and Other Stories* (1988), a book of Bharati Mukherjee dealing entirely with the immigrant experience. Entitled "The Management of Grief," it is a fictional account of some Canadians of Indian origin, who have lost their close relatives in the Air India jumbo jet disaster off the coast of Ireland. It is significant that the flight originated in Canada, and was on its way to India. The majority of the travellers were Indians. Being an India-born herself, Bharati Mukherjee expresses the sense of grief of those left behind in Canada more authentically than any native Canadian, American or British writer could. The outlook of one of the characters in the story is pointedly Indian: "Kusum says we can't escape our fate. She says that all those people—our husbands, my boys, her girl with the nightingale voice, all those Hindus, Christians, Sikhs, Muslims, Parsis, and atheists on that plane—were fated to die together off this beautiful bay."[1] Again, note what the narrator, Shaila Bhave, says: "I am trapped between two modes of knowledge. At thirty-six I am too old to start over and too young to give up. Like my husband's spirit, I flutter between worlds." (189)

Another Mukherjee character, Panna Patel, in "A Wife's story" complains, "In my red silk sari I'm conspicuous." (25) This is a conclusion corroborated by Meera Shastri, an Indian immigrant in Canada, in her essay, "Canadian Experience": "Within a week of my arrival in Toronto, I realized that the sari was not a practical outfit for the Canadian winter and took to wearing pants. It was just a short while before I began to feel self-conscious about wearing saris even when the weather was good."[2] Numerous similar observations are reflected in the experiences and writings of Canadian writers of fiction of Indian origin.

Neil Bissoondath, V.S. Naipaul's sister's son, is a West Indian of the East Indian origin. He was born in Trinidad and went in 1973 to Toronto to complete a degree in French at the York University. He stayed on to live and writes in Canada. For obvious reasons, his fiction carries the triple flavour of his diverse backgrounds. *Digging up the Mountains* (1985) is a collection of short stories in which he examines the intellectual implications of the motifs of changing places and exchanging cultures. This reminds one of the manner in which Naipaul tackles these themes in some of his early fictional works dealing with the life of the East Indian immigrants in Trinidad. In one of his essays, Bissoondath refers to the Canadian oil company executive, who was looking for an apartment in Toronto. This man rejected buildings with East Indian tenants because he believed that cockroaches were symbols of good luck in their culture. Such misunderstandings persist and give us some idea of what an author is up against while transforming immigrant experience into fiction.

Nazneen Sadiq was born in Kashmir in 1944. She went to Canada when she was twenty, and stayed on to write fiction that has the flavour of her immigrant experience. Her *Ice Bangles* (1988) is a collection of short stories. In the title story, Naila, the narrator, living in Canada, goes home to attend the wedding of her brother. It comes as a surprise to her that her brother's bride, though quite charming, is dark-skinned. Her comment in this regard is revealing: "The fair-skinned northerners had practised for centuries the same discrimination which their British masters had been accused of. Her mother, who had hoped secretly for a Kashmiri wife for her only son, had been cheated." (*Between Worlds,* 31) When Naila notices the children of the domestic servants peeping over the boundary walls at the glittering festivities; "She was conscious for the first time of social divisions and found them disturbing. Five years of living in Canada had awakened a social conscience which emerged with the embarrassment of adolescent acne." (34)

So far I have referred to three writers of fiction, who coming with their Indian and other backgrounds write about the immigrant experience in Canada, drawing very much on their first hand experience. They highlight the problems of immigrants confronted with the situation of living in the midst of an alien culture. It creates more problems for them when they go back, even though temporarily, to the places of their birth. Now I would like to draw your attention to a Canadian writer of Indian origin, who, while living in his adopted home, writes most authentically about his experience in India before going to Canada.

Rohinton Mistry, a Parsi, was born in Bombay in 1952, and immigrated to Canada in 1975. For ten years, he worked in a bank, studying English and philosophy part time at the University of Toronto. His first short story fetched him a Hart Home Prize for fiction in 1983. His stories have been published in major Canadian literary journals and anthologies. *Such a Long Journey* (1991) is a brilliant first novel by one of the most remarkable writers of fiction to have emerged from India in recent years. It is set in Bombay against the backdrop of the Indo-Pakistan of 1971 and the emergence of Bangladesh as a separate independent nation. The novel tells the story of a Parsi bank official, Gustad Noble, and the peculiar way in which the conflict in the Indian sub-continent affects him and his family.

The remarkable thing about *Such a Long Journey* is its absolute Indianness, without any trace of the Canadian immigrant experience that the author must have gone through for fifteen years before the publication of the book. It is steeped in the atmosphere of Bombay, particularly of the exclusive Parsi community of that city. The Khodadad Building, an apartment house, where Gustad Noble lives along with his Parsi neighbours, is a world in itself. Dilnavaz, his wife, is beset by the usual Indian superstitions, encouraged by Miss Kutpitia, the mysterious spinster. When Sohrab, the elder son of Gustad, refuses to join the IIT, against the wishes of his father, and leaves home, Dilnavaz circles a lemon over his head, offering the juice of it in a sweetened drink to the half-wit Tehmul-Lungraa. For general good luck, she hangs a lemon and some green chilies on a string above the front door from inside. Again, she consults Miss Kutpitia, when baffled by the prolonged illness of her daughter, Roshan, in order to devise ways of warding off the evil eye. The world of Indian superstition in *Such a Long Journey* is far removed from the western society of Toronto in Canada, where Rohinton Mistry wrote the novel.

Mistry shows an Indian's knowledge about corruption being an ingrained part of life at all levels in India. He reiterates how an ordinary citizen can get nothing done without bribes, if he has any dealings with the municipality, the police department or the politicians. Dr. Paymaster, family physician of Gustad Noble, points out: "that municipal corruption was only a microcosmic manifestation of the greed, dishonesty and moral turpitude that flourished at the country's centre. He described meticulously how, from the very top, whence all power flowed, there also dripped the pus of putrefaction, inflicting every society below."[3]

Mistry reminds us how goods donated by people to support the war effort at the time of the Chinese invasion later turned up for sale in the Chor Bazaar. He makes critical references to Indira Gandhi's handling of the Bangladesh War. The episode of Nagarwala cheating the State Bank of India of several lakhs of rupees, by impersonating the Prime Minister on the phone, is woven into the fabric of the novel and intermingled with the fate of Major Bilimoria, a friend of Gustad Noble. A notable concern in *Such a Long Journey* is the raw deal that Bilimoria gets from the Government out of working for the RAW. Gustad gets involved in the shady deal and draws his friend, Dinshawji, too into it. The death of Dinshawji from cancer is a high point in the novel, as it reveals the truly noble side of Gustad, who is the sole male mourner at the Parsi funeral rites that follow. It is a kind of cleansing process that pushes Gustad very close to an intense spiritual experience.

Gustad's dream of launching his son as a successful engineer is a lofty one, and a purely Indian one at that. "The dream of IIT took shape, then took hold of their imaginations. And the Indian Institute of Technology became the Promised Land. It was El Dorado and Camelot, it was Xanadu and Oz. It was the home of the Holy Grail." (66) One cannot fail to appreciate the tongue-in-cheek flavour of this passage.

To his young daughter's question, "Daddy, why is West Pakistan killing the people in East Pakistan?" (81) Gustad can offer only this simplistic answer: "East Pakistan is poor, they said to West, we are always hungry, please give us a fair share. But West said no. Then East said, in that case we don't want to work with you. So, as punishment, West Pakistan is killing and burning East Pakistan." (81) That is as close a summation of the political upheaval as any.

Peerbhoy Paanwala in *Such a Long Journey* is an institution by himself. He has a *paan* for all seasons, but the one most in demand is the bed-breaker or *palungtode paan* with its renowned aphrodisiacal properties. Possessing a rich faculty for myth-making, Peerbhoy suggests that even the Moghul emperors used this variety of *paan* when they went to their harems. To young boys, he would offer *a paan* which would cleanse their heads of boyish impurities and help them concentrate on their studies. When the Bangladesh war is at its apex, Peerbhoy rises to great heights in weaving a myth about the doings of Gen. Yahya Khan and his military governor of East Pakistan.

Gustad Noble's dreams and expectations are modest indeed, but circumstances prevailing in the India of his times conspire to deny him even these. It is very hard on him that he cannot make things happen in such a way as to fulfil his aspirations. Forces, stranger than himself, come in the way of his achieving his ambitions. His elder son does not join the IIT; Roshan, his favourite child, suffers from a prolonged illness; Dinshawji, his best friend, dies of cancer; and another friend, Bilimoria, betrays his trust. Gradually, Gustad Noble modifies his dreams and dilutes his expectations. It is quite obvious that he is not in control of things. But this does not make him turn into a defeatist. In the true oriental way, his triumph consists in the calm manner with which he faces each trial of his life. It lies in his acceptance of the harsh realities of the world to which he belongs. His grandest moment comes towards the end of the novel, when he forgives his erring son, and clasps him to his bosom in a noble gesture of acceptance of Sohrab's decision to lead his own life.

The conclusion that I would like to draw in this brief essay relates to the various ways in which the immigrant writers of Indian origin in Canada convert their experience into fiction. Few among them would opt to project their newly acquired western values, which perhaps they fail to appreciate fully. Some, like Bharati Mukherjee and Nazneen Sadiq, concentrate on the changes in the attitudes and sensibility of their fictional characters, when confronted with the dilemmas of cross-cultural concerns. This is, no doubt, a rewarding way of projecting the Indian immigrant experience in Canada. But we should not underestimate the contribution of writers of fiction like Rohinton Mistry, who open a window on India for their Canadian and other western readers. *Such a Long Journey* tells us more about the Parsi community in Bombay than a book of sociology possibly could. What is more, Mistry is able to project the emotional life and personal relationships of the Parsis as a valuable part of the wider human experience at the international level by writing about these things from across worlds. The Indian readers of Mistry will react to this book in their own way. For them, he presents an interesting slice of their own life, which for them is a most valued thing. While Salman Rushdie, another Indian expatriate writer, offends with his satiric denunciations, Rohinton Mistry entertains while he exposes the frailties of his characters with his gentle humour and an eye for the comic in human nature.

NOTES

1. Bharati Mukherjee, *The Middleman and Other Stories* (Penguin Books India, 1990), p. 184.
2. Milly Charon, ed., *Between Two Worlds: The Canadian Immigrant Experience* (Montreal: Nu-Age Editions, 1988), p. 284.
3. Rohinton Mistry, *Such a Long Journey* (London: Faber and Faber, 1991), pp. 312-13.

Discourses of Displacement: South Asian Voices from Canada

CHARU C. MISHRA
K.G. Arts and Science College, Raigarh

Culture clash, the process and resulting guilt of fleeing a restrictive background or tradition, the problem of being displaced from one's own culture and finding oneself in a totally new environment, these are problems for growing numbers of individuals in today's world. In such a situation where the individual is seen as geographically culturally, linguistically or sometimes psychologically estranged, the whole question of individual's identity becomes an unattainable ideal. The South Asian Canadian fiction, especially from the writers of Asian, Caribbean or African origin, abundantly reflects these anxieties, the sense of dislocation and alienation of individuals caught in a world of conflicting values.

Canada, a nation with "too much geography" and "no particular history," poses a grave challenge to all immigrants, that of charting a "cultural territory" of one's own or be doomed with a hyphenated identity forever. In this regard, the South Asian writers in Canada, especially those from the third world countries, have been a discriminated lot as it was considered to be a white nation, the nation of the French and the British. It's only after the official acceptance of Canada as a multicultural country that this tension between being white and non-white has eased to some extent. However, in their initial stage of writing, writers like Vassanji had to face considerable resistance before being accepted by the Canadian literary milieu. The advent of literary theories like post-colonialism and feminism have provided added advantage to the Third World writers in Canada in charting out their own "cultural territory."

While explaining the role of immigrant writer, Stella Sandahl writes: "He is the one who can convey experiences from different worlds, being himself part of different worlds. Complexity does not mean schizophrenia. We can and should contribute to the common culture and still remain ourselves."[1]

In this regard, the Third World writer's contribution to contemporary Canadian literature is quite noteworthy. Large-scale decolonisation, a post-imperial climate and an increasing temper since the 1960s have provided a milieu for the expatriate writers, to be part of the international literary scene. Living in Canada, expatriate writers like Neil Bissoondath, M.G. Vassanji, Michael Ondaatji, Bharati Mukherjee, Rohinton Mistry, to name a few, are paradigmatic of the polycultural quality of contemporary literatures and have helped evolve what may be called a transnational literature. Expatriate writing, born out of the dialectic between displacement and relocation, belonging and alienation raises theoretical formulations which provide fresh perspectives to creative works.

In an interview with Bruce Meyer, Neil Bissoondath talked of his personal experiences regarding the clash of cultural values in the following manner:

> I grew up in a culture that restricted me, a culture that imposed its values on me and that had little regard for my personal feelings and desires. From this point of view, I identify with that Japanese girl (in "The Cage") very closely—the girl can't escape her past. When I left Trinidad, I knew I was leaving for good—the girl in this story was incapable of saying that.

Like Bissoondath, other immigrant writers too reflect these sentiments and desires of individuals displaced geographically and culturally in their works.

In this paper I shall make a comparative assessment of the following stories: Neil Bissoondath's "The Cage," Bharati Mukherjee's "A Wife's Story," M.G. Vassanji's "Leaving"[2] and Rohinton Mistry's "Lend Me Your Light."[3] While analyzing the theme of displacement and alienation undergone by the characters in the process of their physical and psychological adaptation to the new environment, I shall also attempt to compare the above paradigms from the perspective of male and female experiences in relation to the diasporic or expatriate experience of each author.

Michi, the female protagonist of Bissoondath's "The Cage" grows up in the four walls of a patriarchal Japanese culture which imposes its restrictive values on every woman in the name of tradition. Michi and her mother are the subjects of this dominating culture, which guards every move of female members, even impinges upon their privacy to secure its hold. Bissoondath presents the mother and the daughter in contrast to bring out the difference of attitude of two generations. While her mother meekly and unquestioningly accepts the cultural dictum, Michi brews up her resistance deep within, unable to give in like her mother.

She is virtually non-existent for her father till she was fifteen. Suddenly his interest in her grows since he is responsible to transplant the cultural values in her. Learning music lessons, keeping away from boys, mixing up with people only of their status are some of the important things she was taught to do. When a simple letter from a boy was taken away from her, she realizes how she has no hold even over her own life:

> I learnt, more than anything else, how little of my life was my own, in my father's eyes. His claim to my privacy finally caused me to regard him with eyes of ice. (82)

On her father's advice, she took a course on dietetics and she was even told to court men chosen by him. In order to evade this cage formed by patriarchal culture she leaves for Toronto, an uncommon Japanese destination that would provide her anonymity and freedom from the restrictive bondage of culture.

Once away from her homeland, Michi is able to view the old and the new culture properly and attempts to "place" herself. Her initial reaction is to watch the people of the new land, the "glimpses of lives I would never touch." But gradually she acquaints herself with the inmates of her apartment house and encounters the nuances of both the cultures through their subtle hints. On her way to school, she finds people displaying themselves at the sidewalks and is irked by their behaviour demanding to be noticed. More than this, her English Tutor's insistence that she never ate bread in Japan suggests the baseless bias the western people hold for the oriental food habit:

> He insisted that I, being a Japanese person, never ate bread, only rice and vegetables and raw fish and nothing else. He would not believe that I had tasted my first big mac in Tokyo. (94)

Marvelling at the immensity of freedom that Toronto would hold for her, she reflects:

> Toronto: a place where my personality could be free, it was not a city of traditions in a country of traditions. It was America, in the best implication that word held for us. Japanese: bright, clean, safe, new. Life experienced without the constraints of an overwhelming past. (95)

But her dream of freedom without constraints is short lived. Her relationship with the third floor neighbour Sherry shocks her enough to see the tangibility of her belogingness. She worked as a stripper and a call girl. Unaware of this, one night, hearing some grunting noise from her room, she calls on her like any sensible neighbour. But to her utter dismay, Sherry accuses her of being a moron, one too stupid to understand the other culture and its practices. Through her acquaintance with Mrs. Duncan and her landlady Mrs. Harris, she comes to the realization that women are displaced everywhere, as much in Canada as in Japan. For Mrs. Harris and Mrs. Duncan, both widows, keeping their husband's name and not their own is tradition:

> "It is tradition, dear, Christian tradition."
> "Yes, dear, it is as simple as that. It's what women have always done." (98)

Michi discovers from her mother's letter that "Michi" her grandmother being "a strong and independent woman with her own ideas" had been beaten to submission and finally left with only a grandson (her father) as an outlet for her sense of life. She is now confronted with the past that she has tried to ignore in Toronto. She has by now seen that it is better to have a room of one's own than have nothing. Her final decision to return to her father's house and arrange flowers only provokes the reader to see her desperate attempt to "place" herself even if through a cage-like tradition. Despite her realization that "the corollary of tradition's pride is tradition's guilt" (99) her nonresistance to patriarchal culture would impel any feminist critic to comment that Bissoondath's inclination still lies towards a male-oriented society.

While Bissoondath allows Michi to return to her past tradition, Panna Bhatt in Bharati Mukherjee's "A Wife's Story" is caught between the two worlds. After her son's death, she leaves for New York to pursue a Ph.D. course and distances herself from her husband. Her reaction to the racial discrimination and prejudiced language in David Mamet's play *Glengarry Glen Ross* brings out her sense of indignity and outrage:

> It's the tyranny of American dream that scares me. First you don't exist. Then you are invisible. Then you are funny. Then you are disgusting. Insult, my American friends will tell me, is a kind of acceptance. No instant dignity here. I long, at times, for clear-cut answers. Offer me instant dignity, today and I'll take it. (422)

Panna's husband works in Laxmi Cotton Mills, a private enterprise in Ahmedabad. With the end of family responsibility, now she is virtually a different self. She had almost overcome her inhibition of her past life, even sexually she feels no compunction to share with her male friends like Imre, a Muslim from Hungary. Her transitional state and the extent of her dislocation comes to the forefront when her husband arrives in New York on holiday for fifteen days. During his presence, she keeps herself away from other friends. But on meeting Imre, she feels as if she is really seeing him for the first time: "Guilt, shame, loyalty. I long to be ungracious, not ingratiate myself with both men." (428)

Being in such a transitional state, she finds herself too far away from her past culture and tacitly rejects her husband's suggestion to go back home. She further reflects: "Tonight I should make up to him for my years away, the gutted trucks, the degree I'll never use in India. I want to pretend with him that nothing has changed." (432)

Ironically, her plea to stay back for study is meaningless. It only suggests her confused state, her in "in-between" position where she is vacillating between two cultures preventively conforming to the past, yet looking forward to the present. Mukherjee has beautifully presented her character "in transition" who is seeking possibilities and desires that conflict with her past and her present ideals. "A Wife's Story" is an exemplary statement on the new "international person" who is attempting to balance heritage with new situations quite like her writer.

Vassanji's protagonist Aloo in "Leaving" is a boy from the Indian Community settled in Dar es Salaam in Tanzania whose sole reason for immigration is to better the economic condition of his family through foreign education. His ambition to be a doctor is thwarted by the handiwork of some corrupted bureaucrat who selects him for a course on Agriculture. This denial of opportunity sets in the dislocation spirit in Aloo, which is inflamed by his mother through her humour and joke. For Aloo, it is only the American University, that can fulfil his promise, give him a "place": "A whole universe was out there waiting for him if only he could reach it." (492)

His selection in California Institute of Technology virtually sets him on the course of dislocation from his native culture and attracts him to look forward to the new culture hopefully. His letter from London during his brief stopover there evocatively brings out the significance of the present place and the inadequacy of his native land:

> Oh London it seemed that it would never end—blocks and blocks of houses, squires, parks, monuments—could any city be larger?—How many of our Dar es Salaams would fit here, in this one gorgeous city. (495)

Aloo leaves for USA with promises to his mother that he would not "marry a white woman" and would not "smoke or drink." Whether or not he chooses to keep his promise is not the contentious issue here. However, such foreclosure hints at the possible displacement he would undergo in the new culture while abiding to the restrictive values of the past imposed upon him. Vassanji quite subtly brings out the differences and tensions between the First world and Third world and the manner in which colonial past influences the ways in which postcolonial nations and nationals view themselves and their aspirations.

Rohinton Mistry's "Lend Me Your Light" when compared to the above three stories seems to be the most poignant in reflecting the dichotomies confronting his characters who are trying desperately to hold both the worlds in balance. While Jamshed and Kersi immigrate to New York and Toronto respectively, Percy, the brother of Kersi, stays back in India. It may be pointed out here that both Vassanji and Mistry choose representatives from their own community to reinforce the idea of their typical culture.

Percy's schoolmate Jamshed hails from a rich family who virtually is an alien even among his class fellows by eating his school lunch, in the "leather-upholstered luxury of the backseat" of his "chauffeur-driven, air-conditioned family car." (99) All this hyphenated lavishness only increases the distance between him and the culture he lives in. For him his displacement is rooted in his belief that all races in India are "Ghatis" who are flooding all the places, leaving none for Parsis like him. Jamshed represents that breed of affluent Parsi family who believed in extending the colonial authority in absence of their erstwhile colonial masters. The post-Independence India holds no future for such bigot residue of imperialism. "Absolutely no future in this stupid place. Bloody corruption everywhere. And you can't buy any of the things you want, don't even get to see a decent English movie. First chance I get, I'm going abroad. Preferably the U.S." (178)

Jamshed manages to leave for the U.S., his land of promises that can provide him his much-needed "Place." After him, it is Kersi's turn to leave for Toronto, though his reason for immigration is to better his and his family's economic standard. His relationship with his brother Percy reflects his alienation in his own family. While for Percy his idealist goal to free rural India from poverty and oppression roots him strongly to his place, for Kersi "there weren't any prospects in this country." (178) Leaving for Toronto with severe infection of conjunctivitis, he half-jokingly compares himself with displaced Tiresias, "blind and throbbing between two lives, the one in Bombay and the one to come in Toronto." (180)

More than a year after his departure from India, Jamshed's anguish and contempt for his old place seems to lessen in no way though no longer he lives in it. "Bombay is horrible, seems dirtier than ever, and the whole trip just made me sick. I had my fill of it in two weeks and was happy to leave." (181)

Though Kersi is not so bitter about his old place, he too is undergoing a crisis in Toronto where he finds the whole community living the life they have left behind in India and relishing its food still. He keeps his feelings off from Jamshed yet he concurs to his complaints internally. Both of them show no sign of adapting to the new culture and find a place of their own. It is Percy who sees Jamshed's torments and agony of displacement in his desperate assertion of authority over the waiter in the five star Taj Mahal hotel before his friends: "Explaining that this was the only way to handle incompetence. Indians were too meek and docile, and should learn to stand for their rights the way people do in States." (185)

Like Jamshed Kersi confesses of his displacement in India in his inability to board the local train amidst the milling crowd: "With the old and the feeble was my place, as long as I was a tourist hero, and not committed to life in the combat zone." (188) He dares not fight for his old place in it while Jamshed vents his anger on the stall owners of Flora fountain to release his frustration of dislocation: "Terrible isn't it, the way these buggers think they own the streets—don't even leave you enough room to walk." (190)

The final encounter of the three characters brings out the sense of dislocation and belongingess by presenting in contrast the immigrants and the one living in India. Percy returns from the village, shocked by the murder of his friend Navjeet by village landlord. Jamshed urges him in his characteristic off-handish manner to go to States where "if you're good at something you are appreciated, and you get ahead." Ironically this knowledge of his has found him no place there. While rooted in his idealism and faith, Percy prepares himself for his next strategic move to village, Kersi returns to Toronto as confused as before: "I Tiresias, throbbing between two lives, humbled by the ambiguities and dichotomies confronting me." (192)

Kersi comes to the realization that like him Jamshed is also torn by his unfulfilled desire to locate himself somewhere: "Was he, too, waiting for some epiphany and growing impatient because without it life in America was bewildering? Perhaps the contempt and disdain which he shed was only his way of lightening his own load." (192) Jamshed's "confusion, disdain and arrogance" is the surfacing of Kersi's "entire burden of riddles, and puzzles unsolved." (192)

Like Mistry, his characters reflect the anxiety of his community that has undergone the difficulties of Diaspora. In the post-Independence India, the Persi community's looking westward for carving out another "cultural territory" seems to be the reason for their dislocation. Mistry like Vassanji brings out the ambiguities and dichotomies confronting his dislocated characters quite dexterously. It is through such analysis of male and female experiences that the discourses of displacement of the above Immigrant writers could be read in a new perspective.

In *The Third World Novel of Expatriation*, Viney Kirpal states: "For modern or traditional, it is the eternal quest of man to seek to put down roots somewhere, to possess some point of space to which he can relate emotionally or psychologically." (45) The need to establish one's roots becomes more acute in the case of transcultural writers like those discussed here, who shuffle between both physical and psychological borders of two different cultures. This "in-between" position invests expatriate writing with the tension of binary polarities as "dislocation vs. relocation, domicile vs. diasporic consciousness, dispossession vs. integration, heritage vs. hybridity and exile vs. involvement."[4] Discourses such as these are creative expressions of the lived experience of the immigrant writers that also lend insight into the existential realities of geographical displacement.

NOTES

1. Stella Sandahl, "South Asian Literature: A Linguistic Perspective," *A Meeting of Streams*, ed. M.G. Vassanji (Toronto: TSAR, 1985).
2. Neil Bissoondath, "The Cage," M.G. Vassanji, "Leaving," Bharati Mukherjee, "A Wife's Story," *Contemporary Short Fiction Written in English*, ed. Bruce Meyer (Scarborough, Ontario: Prentice-Hall Canada, 1997).
3. Rohinton Mistry, "Lend Me Your Light," "Swimming Lessons," *Firozsha Baag* (New York: Vintage International Edition, Random House, 1997).
4. C. Vijayasree, "The Politics and Poetics: The Indian Versions," *Interrogating Post Colonialism: Theory, Text and Context*, ed. Harish Trivedi and Meanakshi Mukherji (Shimla: IAAS, 1996), p. 221.

Silencing of Women across the Globe: A Study of Suniti Namjoshi's *The Feminist Fables*

SUMITA PURI
Dyal Singh (E) College
University of Delhi

> 'But what would you do if you were the Red Queen?'
> 'I would make everybody behave themselves,' Alice said firmly.
> 'How?'
> 'Well,' began Alice . . .
>
> (Suniti Namjoshi, 1991)

Introducing Suniti Namjoshi as a writer of the Indian Diaspora presently settled in England would only serve as a cursory sketch of the creator of a vast range of poetry, fables, and fiction. In fact, the large number of her works marked by her alternate forms, open-mindedness and unorthodox standpoint make her a writer opposed to all forms of classification and categorization. Her abandonment of authoritative positions and her decision to lead an unconventional life facilitate her personal and creative growth. Rejection of prestigious positions led her to investigate the nature of all modes of dominance—of class, race, gender and nationality and to transgress them. This transgression becomes her key concern and with stylistic wit and inventiveness, she offers the readers a non-conformist and deviant world through her works. Born in Bombay, in India, in 1941, Suniti Namjoshi joined the Indian Administrative Service in 1964, but soon left it. She went on to pursue a Master's Degree in Public Administration at University of Mussourie, Columbia. She completed her thesis on Ezra Pound and left Toronto in 1987 to permanently settle down with her lesbian partner, Gillian Hanscombe, in Devon, England.

A poet, fabulist, mythmaker, fiction writer, feminist and a lesbian in the same breath, Suniti Namjoshi began her literary career with a book of poetry *Poems* published by the Writers Workshop, Calcutta in 1967. After this, she published numerous poems, fables, articles and reviews in India, Canada, United States and Britain. Poems was followed by *Cyclone in Pakistan* and *More Poems* in 1971, also published in India. She then wrote *The Jackass and the Lady* in Canada between 1972 and 1976, which was published in India. Her first work published outside India was a collection of poems about death and childhood grief, *The Authentic Lie* in 1982. *Feminist Fables* (1981) and *The Conversations of Cow* (1985) were published in London. *Feminist Fables* is a prose work containing fables with animals and figures from Western and Indian fables and folklore, teaching human beings lessons regarding their behaviour and actions. *The Conversations of Cow* concerns freewheeling identities of a lesbian cow named Bhadravati transforming into a woman, a white man and a Hindu goddess.

Retelling traditional tales to propose her feminist agenda becomes the prime motif of *Feminist Fables*, which picks up several voices—of Cinderella, Rapunzel and the Red Riding Hood and of *From the Bedside Book of Nightmares* with voices of Caliban, Prospero, Miranda, Antigone and Penelope to comment on the victimization of women in heterosexual patriarchal supremacy. In 1986, Namjoshi published a collection of poetry *Flesh and Paper* to give voice to her lesbian reality. *The Blue Donkey Fables* followed in 1980 that contained fables full of animals—the blue donkey, the one-eyed monkey, the magpie and others to satirize human frailties and weaknesses. *Because of India: Selected Poems and Fables* and *The Mothers of Maya Diip* were published in London in 1989. The former is divided into ten sections, including poems and prose fables and the author's comments and views on them. *The Mothers of Maya Diip* finally introduces us to her vision of a feminist utopia, a dream of a matriarchal world where goodwill, peace and sisterhood will prevail. Apart from these, she has written *Aditi and the One-Eyed Monkey* (1986) and *Saint Suniti and the Dragon*

(1994). *Building Babel* (1996) and *Goja: An Autobiographical Myth* (2000) are her latest contributions to the literary scene.

Suniti Namjoshi's *The Feminist Fables* is a result of Canadian feminist ideals interwoven with the Indian heritage. Unlike traditional tales, where generalizations are applied to individuals, Namjoshi's fables address idiosyncratic individuals in particular idiosyncrasies. Unlike traditional fables, most of her characters are females advocating revolt against the system. Her fables have a feminist rendition and rewriting them enables her to reveal what is unsaid and undermined in the patriarchal hegemony rooted in traditional fables. Therefore, they offer a new vision into the condition of women in a male dominated world. Through inventing a new mythology, they question the oppression of women in patriarchy and suggest alternatives. Savita Goel, in her article on *Feminist Fables*, comments: "In these hilarious, witty and elegantly written fables, she [Namjoshi] has invented a mythology that is simultaneously thought-provoking and entertaining and deals with the aspects of women's lives that have been erased, ignored, demeaned and mystified."[1] Through the rewriting of fables and fairy tales, she theorizes that heterosexuality and patriarchy ascribe negative and passive roles to women by holding their tongues. By transgression of gender constructs, women can liberate themselves from suppression and discover their real strength. Since male dominance restricts them, it should be overthrown completely. Her radical views are fully articulated in her utopian model of a matriarchal world where men are extremely insignificant and incapable.

If fables and myths are used for serving pedagogical needs, Namjoshi "uses this essentially moralizing and instructive genre in a satiric way," and "sets herself against the 'truths' of a given order."[2] A fable is linked to the proverb that claims to be a universal repository of truths. Hence, it becomes essential that fables depict types, not individuals. But her fables break the very notion of cultural stereotypes of the masculine and the feminine. Her three-fold marginalization of being a lesbian woman writer of the Indian Diaspora is clearly reflected in her fables where she develops the "Asian perspective," the "alien perspective," and the "lesbian perspective."[3] Her fables, therefore, are set apart from the traditional ones and express the hidden "truths" of the latter by exposing the patriarchal hegemony embedded in them. In *Because of India*, she reports that for her, the fables "were a way of exploring feminist ideas and their implications for the patterns I had inherited through the mainstream literary tradition."[4]

The two essential elements of any fable are the presence of non-human characters enacting human behaviour, desires and experiences, and the stating of the moral of the story. Thus, we have non-humans teaching humans lessons in life. As far as this is concerned, Namjoshi's fables also contain birds and beasts tutoring human beings. Her characters range from animals such as ducks, swans, lizards, monkeys, crocodiles, mares, snakes, mongooses, bears, ostriches, foxes and owls to mythical characters such as Red Riding Hood, Little Miss Muffet, Jack of the Beanstalk, Goldilocks and the Ugly Duckling to invented ones like the handsome young dyke, the New Woman and the Incredible Woman. In an interview with Chelva Kanaganayakam, she says:

> I am always asked why I write fables and why I write about animals. I try to supply answers, but the honest truth is I don't know. We don't separate animals from human beings. As for animals talking, why not?[5]

What are the issues raised in the fables? How does Suniti Namjoshi bring to the fore the ill treatment faced by women? If one looks at the fables closely, one may find them as an explication of the three phases denominated by Elaine Showalter—the 'Feminine,' the 'Feminist' and the 'Female.' The fables explore the 'feminine' aspects in women, where they succumb to the wishes of men and comply with the dominant modes of behaviour dictated to them; the 'feminist' phase where they protest against the values and demand autonomy and power; the 'female' phase where they call women to search for their identity. The fables point out that the inequality between sexes is not a biological but a cultural construct. Gender differences are constructed consciously for empowerment of women and Namjoshi's fables deconstruct these differences and identities as well.

Patriarchy has relegated women to a subordinate status in family and society. They have been ordered to be passive, docile and submissive. Their position has been confined to the household as obedient servants of men. The first fable "From the Panchatantara" is a story of a Brahmin who prays to Lord Vishnu for a son but gets a daughter instead. Still, he imparts all his knowledge to her to make her a Brahmin. After much meditation Lord Vishnu reappears and the Brahmin again asks for a son. In his next birth, the Brahmin becomes a woman and bears eight sons. Namjoshi ends the tale on a satiric note that sums up the entire collection. This time the girl asks for a human status and the god sneaks away with saying, "Ah, that is much harder."[6] With skilful irony, the author reveals that women have been denied human status and human rights.

Often Namjoshi's fables are pithy and concise and end on a crisp note that implies what she wants to say. In exposing the status of a wife in a male-governed society, "The Tale of Two Brothers" is a perfect citation. I would like to quote the small fable fully to illustrate my view:

> There was once a man who thought he could do anything, even be a woman. So he acquired a baby, changed its diapers and fed the damn thing three times a night. He did all the housework, was deferential to men, and got worn out. But he had a brother, Jack Cleverfellow, who hired a wife, and got it all done. (36)

The fable clearly states that women are reduced to servants in the house. Their space is restricted to the home where performing the household chores, taking care of the children and being obeisant to men become their only duty.

Traditional fables contain animals wearing the human garb and enacting their conduct. Namjoshi's fables also contain numerous animals and beasts stating feminist ideas and morals. In a scoffing tale "No Frog in Her Right Mind" the fabulist pictures the immurement of women in a patriarchal set-up. The fable is about a prince who catches a female frog while playing and takes it home. At home, he puts her in a jar and all nightlong the frog struggles to escape. Her efforts succeed and she flees at dawn. The prince gets up in the morning and, not finding the frog in her place, goes outside carrying the jar. The title of the fable suggests that the frog's attempt to defy the norms and move out of her defined space are futile as the prince would trap her again. Women have grappled hard to move out of their homes in search of freedom, yet men have fettered them by displaying their manhood over them.

The height of subordination is brought out in "Her Mother's Daughter" in which there is a couple who has a feminist daughter. As the daughter grows up, she decides to avenge the wrongs done on her mother. The mother is shocked as subservience is rooted in her psyche and the idea of going against the said norms is almost irrational for her. The daughter tries hard to explain to her mother that patriarchy has made them dependent on the father and that they should fight for their liberation. The horrified mother makes it clear to the daughter that, "in a good patriarchy the women are dependent, but they're not allowed to know it," and "that's how it should be." (96)

Namjoshi's fables allege that daughters are trained from childhood itself to be passive, patient, and complaisant and to "hold their tongues." The first instance of this is shown in the fable "The Lesson" where a young girl after being inspired by the naked emperor in the noted fairy tale of "The Emperor's Clothes" undresses herself and believes that she is an emperor. Her mother, at once, chides her and gives her the right lesson which is given to all the daughters in a patriarchal society:

> Don't be silly, darling. Only little boys grow up to be Emperors. As for little girls, they marry Emperors; and they learn to hold their tongues, particularly on the subject of the Emperor's clothes. (8)

Patriarchy makes women extremely vulnerable to objectification and commodification, as they are acquiescent and not willing to protest. Namjoshi unveils this aspect of patriarchal autonomy as well in her fables. In one of the fables, "The Milk-White Mare" set in the times of the Caliph, Prince Haroun-al-Rashid, "defender of the mighty and the protector of the loyal," (27) a woman transformed into a mare by magic is being treated brutally by her husband and father. Earlier, her husband believing her to be a slut had discarded the woman, but now as a mare she was handsome and useful, and was desired by both the men. As long as she is productive, a woman is wanted and is otherwise dumped. Since she was no longer useful for the husband, he threw her out. But as a mare she is profitable and demanded. The Prince does justice: he gives each of them fifty gold pieces and the mare is kept in the stables of the Prince, thus, utilizing her the utmost.

However, in "The Dower" the fabulist tells us that women can revolt against this commodification and enjoy their rights. The fable provides three alternative endings to the main plot. A king desires to have a son but has three daughters in succession. When the first one is born, the queen convinces him that wherever she will walk flowers will sprout. The second is gifted, as where she will walk pearls will be found. But when the third is born the queen dies and the child is not considered to be a real princess, as her gait produced nothing. One day the princess' foot is cut and a ruby is formed out of her blood. Three possible destinies are possible according to the writer: the princess is not supposed to walk with shoes and the king becomes richer and richer; the king marries the unfortunate princess to a poor swineherd before the miracle happens. Once her foot is cut, and the miracle takes place and the couple sells the jewel and gets the princess a new pair of shoes; the first princess becomes a florist, the second sets a pearl business and the third produces a ruby when it suits her.

The heterosexual patriarchal hegemony whereby women are born to provide sexual gratification to men is yet another theme of *Feminist Fables*. "Sheherazade" is one of the *Feminist Fables* where the author plays upon this idea. Men engage themselves in gazing at women and women engage themselves in making themselves apt objects of gaze. Men need to be pleased physically and if women fail to do so they have to pay a price. The fable is narrated as juxtaposing horses with humans, the male sex of both the species overpowering the female physically.

> Watch how the stallion mounts the mare. Watch how the mare submits to the stallion. So the Caliph at night will mount the princess. The princes will give much pleasure to him. This is the law. It pleases Allah. (45)

Once the Caliph is bored with the princess, she will die. The stallion has one thousand mares and the Caliph has one thousand women for their pleasure. In this manner, women have been victims serving men in satisfying all their needs.

Feminist Fables also reveals the classical stereotypes of women in traditional fairy tales and fables. The epithets associated with women are 'stupid,' 'weak,' 'fragile,' 'insipid,' 'demure' and 'imperfect' and 'inferior' to men. In contrast, men are 'rational,' 'brave,' 'strong,' 'bold,' 'flawless' and, undoubtedly, 'superior' of the human species. Wisdom, knowledge and strength are manly qualities alone. In "The Gods," an old couple is gifted with a girl child who is precocious and surpassed everyone in running, music and studies. The gods bless her with great abilities, yet the men of the village are critical of her as " To be so damned good, is not womanly." (37) This is corroborated in "Whore, Bitch, Slut, Sow" in which a strong-minded woman pleads to the Judge that the labels she bore should be changed. The judge tries hard by calling her a thief or a beggar or even a bastard but the scholars argue that she is neither of these:

> 'The truth is, Your Honour,' the scholar replied, 'that her wickedness consists in the fact that she is a woman.' 'Ah,' said the Learned Judge, 'That is the answer. Go away, Woman, that is your name and your new label.' (26)

Having revealed the classical archetypes of the masculine and the feminine in society, Namjoshi shows a stage of protest against this ill treatment. Through her fables, she arouses women to rise out of their slumber and get ready to rebel against patriarchal hegemony. The "Bird Woman" projects this freedom in women where the parents of a she-bird's whose wings begin to grow at a rapid speed refuse to cut them in order to teach her to fly. This action is symbolic of the freedom being given to the bird to fly wherever she wishes. In "Liberation," she transforms herself into a colourless bird to experience freedom. Savita Goel explains the notion of liberty in her fables: "Liberty for her means the deconstruction of social structures, so that they do not retain the shape which men have given them and she is fully aware that the world belongs not only to men but also to women."[7]

The reworking of "Perseus and Andromeda" is also designed at rewriting of the feminine and masculine roles. The traditional fable shows how each time the prince combats with the dragon to save the princess in distress. In Namjoshi's fable the princess has a mind of her own and when tied to the stake, lures the dragon in changing their roles. The dragon becomes the prince, the princess becomes the dragon, and the prince is tied to the stake. The prince is left alone and the dragon and the princess leave. Namjoshi implies that women acquiring an independent status can rid themselves of the constructs of gender laid down by the society.

"Rescued" is the refashioning of Rapunzel's thoughts when she is trapped in the witch's castle. In Namjoshi's fable Rapunzel dreams of the prince coming to rescue her. Displeased with the dream she dreams of liberation in the truest sense:

> She dreams of a castle with a very wide moat and four strong walls and a room of her own where she's perfectly safe. (87)

Freedom from oppression and suppression, from cultural taboos and norms, from patriarchy is the feminist agenda of Namjoshi's fables. The feminist representations of the fairy tales of "Cinderella" and "Hansel and Gretel" contribute to the feminist protest of the fabulist. "And Then What Happened?" tells us that after marrying the Prince, Cinderella realizes that the marriage has not been a fair bargain. The Prince accuses her of having married her for his money and the latter blames him of having done so for her looks. Their marriage is not a just decision and Cinderella walks out. The conventional fairy tale heroine flouts all conventions and bravely decides to end an unhappy marriage. The other tale, "In the Forest," violates gender constructs again, as this time; Gretel is the stronger of the two and confronts the witch whereas Hansel hides behind a tree. Gretel lives with the witch and Hansel goes back to his stepmother, for "when he grows up to be a man, he will fight them all." (93)

Feminist Fables also shows women undergoing a phase of self-discovery. Realizing that they have been victims of oppression in more than one way, women have come a long way in their struggle for emancipation. They have comprehended that their ultimate source of solace and freedom lies outside patriarchy. A lesbian herself, Namjoshi feels that lesbians must be recognized in society and allotted the freedom to exist independently. In her fables, therefore, she promotes the idea of women living with women outside the fetters of patriarchy. She is aware of the indignity attributed to lesbians and she brings this out too in her fables.

The utopian vision of a woman-identified world is most explicitly apparent in "The Moon Shone On." The fable describes the love of two women unable to find words to express their love for each other:

> "I love you," she said in despair to her friend. "And I you," said her friend . . . soon they were entwined in one another's arms. And then? And then the moon shone on, the grass was green, flowers sprouted, it was probably spring, they were lovers after all. (49)

Namjoshi celebrates lesbian identity and consciousness in "The Badge-Wearing Dyke and Her Two Maiden Aunts." Two spinster mice live together and are visited by a niece. The niece wears a number of badges such as: "Gay Liberation is Our Liberation" and "Lesbians Ignite." The two mice comfortably tell their niece that they have been living together for the past twenty-five years. They argue that "on the whole, one is so much more comfortable with one's own sex," (11) and the niece takes off her badges and gives to them.

Thus, *Feminist Fables* exposes the exploitation of women on social, sexual and psychological grounds. The fables reveal the unknowing submission of women in patriarchal dominance and revitalize women to break the bonds that deny them the freedom they deserve. Diane McGifford asserts that "though her fables teach and have animals as teachers, her lessons usurp the status quo to endorse feminine thought . . . and coax the reader to the inevitable conclusion that women have been silenced and men have not."[8] To conclude, Suniti Namjoshi's works posit a hope for a better society based on improved man-woman relationships, resistance to heterosexual and patriarchal oppression, legitimacy for nonconformist sexual relations, realization of women's potential and a sense of belonging to women. The need to validate her radical tenets makes her a writer who refuses to conform to traditional modes of writing and invent new strategies of narration and style. Her exportation of Western and Indian philosophy mingled with wit, jocularity and sarcasm paint a beautiful and more humane world to live in and, therefore, are marked with a celebration of womanhood.

NOTES

1. Savita Goel, "Suniti Namjoshi's *Feminist Fables*: A Minor Feminist Classic," Indian *Women Writers: Critical Perspectives*, ed. J.K. Dodiya and K.V. Surendran (New Delhi: Sarup, 1999), p. 177.
2. Anannya Dasgupta, "'Do I Remove My Skin?': Interrogating 'Identity' in the Fables of Suniti Namjoshi," Unpublished Manuscript, 2001.
3. Suniti Namjoshi, *Because of India: Selected Poems and Fables* (London: Onlywoman Press, 1989), p. 22.
4. Suniti Namjoshi, *Because of India*, p. 79.
5. Chelva Kanaganayakam, *Configurations of Exile: South Asian Writers and Their World* (Toronto: TSAR, 1995), p. 50.
6. Suniti Namjoshi, *Feminist Fables* (India: Penguin, 1995), p. 2.
7. Savita Goel, p. 181.
8. Diane McGifford, "Suniti Namjoshi (1941-)," *Writers of the Indian Diaspora: A Bio-Bibliographical Critical Source Book*, ed. Emmanuel S. Nelson (USA: Greenwood Press, 1993), p. 293.

Indian Diaspora in Rana Bose's "Baba Jacques Dass and Turmoil at Cote-Des-Neiges Cemetery"

S. RAMASWAMY
Bangalore University

Rana Bose, born in Bengal, educated in the United States who moved to Montreal in 1977 is a Founding Member of Montreal Serai and has written and staged nine plays in English. Rana Bose, the Serai's main playwright, is an intellectual who has been influenced by the socialist ideologies of Badal Sircar and Utpal Dutt, and is widely read in literature and political science. In order to assess the South Asian Diaspora, it is necessary to remember that there were two phases of immigration. The first immigrants entered Canada in the earlier half of the twentieth century, majority was of the working class. The Eastern provinces saw an influx of immigrants from South Asia only in the second phase, i.e. 1960 onwards. The second phase consisted of highly educated professionals trained in India. Rana Bose belongs to this later phase.

In addition to the well known "Two Solitudes" in Canada there is now a "Third Solitude"—The Solitude of the South Asian Diaspora. The focus in this paper is on this third solitude with particular reference to Montreal. As Hugh McLennan points out in his novel *The Watch that Ends the Night*:

> It is a curious city, Montreal, and in this story I keep returning to the fact that it is. Strangers never understand its inner nature, and immigrant families, even from other parts of Canada, can live here two generations without coming to know it in *their* bones. I am absolutely certain that Montreal is the subtlest and most intricate city in North America. With her history she could not have been otherwise survived, for here the French, the Scotch and the English,

> over two centuries have been divided on issues which ruin nations and civilizations, yet have contrived to live in outward harmony. This is no accident. They understand certain rules in their bones.[1]

"Baba Jacques Dass and Turmoil at Cote-Dés-Neiges Cemetery"[2] is a remarkable play not only from the point of view of the discussion of diaspora but a very powerful indictment on a number of contemporary issues. There is irony, there is satire, and there is a great deal of anger. Rana Bose can be talked about as the present day 'Angry Young Man.' What John Osborne was to London in 1956, Rana Bose is to Montreal today. The play was successfully staged at the Centaur Theatre in Montreal in 1987. Right away in the first stage direction, the scene is set:

> 5.00 a.m. in the morning. Night sky outline over Montreal. . . . Sound of street traffic, distant siren—drunken yell (Ou est ce que mon miel, hosti) gets closer and louder—till Binoy gets fed up, goes to the window and shouts back: "Regardez, dans i'amoire, cholis!" (175-76)

This establishes the bilingual nature of Montreal. Indeed, one cannot talk about Montreal without the Francophone and Anglophone elements together. At this point a very interesting poem by A.M. Klein entitled "Montreal" which is partly amusing can be referred to exemplifying the bilingual context as the poem is a mixture of both French and English.

> Grand port of navigations, multiple
> The lexicons uncargo'd at your quays,
> Sonnant though strange to me; but chiefest, I,
> Auditor of your music, cherish the
> Joined double-melodied vocabulaire
> Where English vocable and roll Ecossic,
> Mollified by the parle of French
> Bilinguefact your air![3]

In the play under consideration there is a sprinkling of Hindi, representing the presence of the South Asian Diaspora along with French and Spanish. For example, Jacques says "Salud, Salud (Stops in his tracks). Hey, que pasa? Sab thik thak beta?" (188) There are also a number of expressions in Hindi interpolated with English. For example "Bhai bara wrestlingwala chunga joke mar diya." (216) Hindi films are also referred to sarcastically 'Sachcha aur Jhutha'—that was the name of an Indian flick. It means Truth and Bullshit. The language question takes on a humorous turn when Mr. Fraser questions Binoy "Imitating Indian accent." (199) Binoy facetiously "assumes a very Indian accent" (199) purposely:

Mr. Fraser: What is your date of birth?
Binoy: 15th August 1947, Independence Day.
Mr. Fraser: Good, good, Do you speak Hindu?
Binoy: No, sir, but I do speak Hindi and I can of course speak Bengali, some Urdu, Assamese, Oriya. I also know a few words in Gujarati, Marathi and even some Punjabi . . . but as far as the Southern languages go I am not all that conversant. How many languages do you speak?
Mr. Fraser: (bowled over) Well, I'm English Canadian, eh, so I speak English of course Je parle francais, aussi, mais, our (excitedly) I can also speak American, yes (suddenly gets angry) but wait a minute. I am asking the questions. You are the one who has made the application to live in Canada. (199)

The question of immigrants is mentioned in the very first speech of the play. Binoy, the protagonist, says:

> Ramdas, Shiv Pandey's son, sat behind the glass booth, raking every new arrival with relentless questioning. Ramdas from whom girls would run away giggling, the clumsy son-of-a-bitch who drooled from his mouth every time he opened it was now sitting in the glass booth as Canadian Immigration officer! (176)

Binoy, through whom the events in the play unfold themselves is an immigrant who is a writer by profession. About the central character he is creating, Janet his girl friend remarks: "You Indians are so corruptible. Tell me, why does your hero have to be so guilt ridden?" (177) to which Binoy replies: "The big deal Jan is that there is a lot of guilt—guilt is in the minds of the Indian soul, all right—guilt is in the Vedas—guilt is in the Puranas, and by the way it is also Biblical—guilt is rampant." (178) Rana Bose has created an extraordinarily interesting character in Binoy's mother who doesn't understand her son's attitude. However, she has been made thoroughly comic as she is continuously speaking only in well-known proverbs. That is her English. For example, "You're lucky you have a mother . . . a bird in hand is worth." (180) "Giving you advice is like casting pearls at the swine." (180) "You are now scribbling fiction on pieces of yellow paper. Nero fiddles while Rome burns." (181) "What is sport to the cat is death to the rat." (181) "It takes two to tango!" (182) "People in glass houses should not throw bricks at each other." (183) "Those who spit against the wind, spit in their own faces." (184) "As the wind blows so must you set sail." (185) Commenting on her characteristic style, Baba Jacques says:

> She is crazy. I don't ever wanna see her (unsettled) I never wanna see her—one time she told me I run with the hare and hunt with the hounds. What's that mean (Binoy laughs), you're not crazy like her. Do you also speak in proverbs? (190)

Even Janet makes fun of the language of Binoy's mother: "As she says blood runs thicker." (208) Some more examples of Ma's pronouncements are "Well, as they say better late than never." (220) "We should never count the chickens before the eggs are hatched." (220) "One swallow does not make a summer." (220) "I don't let the grass grow under my feet." (220) "Do maggots like rotting flesh?" (231) "You cannot fit a square peg into a round hole." (239) This is one of the devices employed by Rana Bose to create comedy in the play *Baba Jacques*.

The entire Scene V can almost be taken up for a separate discussion where we see Rana Bose at his best when he is describing the cocktail party at an Indian home with all his wit, sarcasm, irony, humour and satire where everything from politics to immigration, petty party talk to the status of Indians abroad is mercilessly assailed. Just one example:

Soni: Aw come on Puri, you've had one too many.
Puri: Oh no! Let me tell you something Soni (licking his lips).
Soni: Oh yeah. Tell me something!
Puri: There's something about this country that is very different.
Soni: What is it?

Puri: I almost don't feel like . . . you know what I mean . . . I don't feel like a . . . like an immigrant any longer.
Soni: What do you feel like?
Puri: Like a Canadian . . . a natural born Canadian—you know it is very sacred feeling . . .
Soni: Like a sacred cow?
Puri: A what?
Soni: A sacred cow.
Puri: The sacred cow, yes . . . important, accomplished and reliable.
Soni: An immigrant cow!
Puri: No a citizen cow in a multicultural Canada.
Soni: Well-fed and respected.
Puri: And tolerated.
Soni: And appreciated. (223)

The party talk also involves the mentioning of an interracial marriage between a Canadian and an Indian. Indian culture subsists on covering up reality—ugliness is cloaked with godliness and spirituality—it is a world of lies." (228) Since it is a cocktail party there is plenty of party talk:

Puri: Arey, Drink it—it is like Mataji's lassi back home!
Woman 1: Mataji's lassi did not have any rum, silly!

At this point Mrs. Tory lets out a very affected laugh and spills some drink on her blouse. Mr. Tory gets some Kleenex and starts wiping her chest. She says "James!" Puri tells Soni: "Alcohol does not leave any stains sir, Bhai, joke maar diya." (211)

Mrs. MP: (a little tipsy—sitting next to Tory MP and laughing loud) You know Mala, what really attracted me to Warren was the fact that he never really wanted to sleep with me before we got married. Now that's what! . . .
Tory MP: (feeling like a wimp) Well! I was kind of wary, you know, because of the rather conservative traditions of Indian culture. (212)
Woman 1: (puts her sari to her nose) Arey chi! chi! Mut bob aur . . . (both start laughing) but what do you think about those two . . . (looks towards Neela).
Woman 2: He is making the moves on her (her eyes flutter).
Woman 1: But he better watch it, cause she will hit him for a home run (both laugh). (227)

As Uma Parameswaran points out: "Montreal and Vancouver are the two major centres of south Asian Canadian theatre but they are quite dissimilar because of their immigration history. . . . The eastern provinces saw an influx of immigrants from South Asia only in the second phase of immigration, 1960s onward. The second phase consisted of highly educated professionals trained in India or in other erstwhile British colonies. . . . Rana Bose's *Baba Jacques Dass and Turmoil at Cote des Neiges Cemetery* is so packed with subtexts that much of it might get lost when staged . . . The Montreal Serai is motivated by forces within the community. They are motivated by patterns of racism endemic to the Canadian system and they react to forces generated by structures outside their heritage culture. Their plays consist of a multicultural cast and deal with problems common to minorities, though examples used are often from the South Asian Canadian experience." (vi-xii)

Binoy the protagonist writer confesses: "I unfold the story of the simple emigration of a middle class family to Canada" (181) to the objection of his mother: "Your father would have turned around six times in his grave if he found out that his only son had taken to a literary career leaving behind a brilliant engineering career." (181) This is significant in the context of how the second wave of emigration consisted of highly educated, technically qualified Indians. The point is further stressed when Binoy's mother points out: "Your father was an M.D. Ph.D. Your sister is a Ph.D., your brother-in-law is no less than a Professor in Biochemistry. Your Nitu uncle is a P. Eng. . . . Your Uncle Belu is also a Ph.D. and has his own company with branch offices in London and Kuwait" (181) to which Binoy replies sarcastically: "My cousin Shubhra is no less. She is teaching genetics at Toronto." (181) This point has been made here to show that the emigrant Indians are very highly qualified intelligentsia and their emigration to Canada as well as to other Western countries indicates an aspect known as "Brain drain." However, Baba Jacques of the title of the play is the other side of the picture. He is a French Canadian who is fascinated by India and who is spiritually oriented. Though Binoy is cynical about this and asks: "Couldn't he for once step out of his little Nirvana in Cote-des-Neige?" (184) Neela is Binoy's sister replies:

> It is not Nirvana (shouting) Binoy, you know, sometimes your arrogance and ignorance appals me! Jacques has nobody he can talk to about his one great passion—which is India—and you! You are neither here in Canada nor there in India, but pretending to be everywhere. There is something about India that is so timeless and without Jacques I would never have known. (184)

There were a number of comments made by Binoy which are severely critical of India. For example:

> Indians have built a poisonous cobweb of ideas around themselves. It is a defence mechanism. If you ask them why everybody is so poor in India, they will say "but culturally we are rich." A virtue is made out of poverty—which the "outsider" can never comprehend. (227)

To give a glimpse of Indians in Canada, just one more defensive remark by Binoy should be quoted:

> You are no less an Indian if you question the immensity of the destitution. If you tell Pun that more than 65% of India's population live below the poverty line—he will say that India has the third largest pool of engineers and technicians in the world. If you tell him why should 300,000 Indian children die every year from measles when a single dose of vaccine costs less than 20 cents, he will say Indian ayurvedists extracted the first blood pressure medicine 2,000 years ago. (228)

Scene II shifts to the Cote-des-Neiges Cemetery. "Night Outline of Montreal Mountain with cross. Bell music. Very dark dim lighting. Like a blue haze. Mysterious. In the background . . . vaults lying side by side with numbers on them. Some tombstones in the background." (185). The play "Baba Jacques" in spite of its stark realism has a surrealistic atmosphere. There are a number of sacrilegious jokes against things Indian by Binoy who is described as an 'agnostic.'

> You know, last night I dreamt I was in the mountains near Rishikesh. I did not see a single sadhu. . . . Actually I was there to

> have my Kundalini rise up in me and shatter through my forehead. (185)
>
> And you may ask me why the hell am I here—do I also suffer from some turmoil? Is it because you've convinced me to resolve the inner shit before I deal with the shit in the outside world? (laughs) And out here suddenly in this fake eeriness in Cote des Neiges cemetery, in Montreal, . . . I've met my destiny. . . . I'm about to give up my rotten materialistic past and join Jacques . . . (laughs) . . . and you my sister you are discovering a spiritual India, an India you were not even born in . . . and through the eyes of who but Jacques again (laughs) Jacques the Quebecois, hippy, fatherless in the eighties, he is our only source of the information on the old country because our parents won't tell us nothing. (186)

There are certain references to political events in India and Canada which are brought together as parallels. For example:

> Jacques: Well . . . you know the October crisis. . . . Trudeau's state of siege.
>
> Binoy: Of course I do, I was already here.
>
> Jacques: Well there was a crisis in India in 75.
>
> Binoy: (Jumps up). Yes of course the Emergency—tell me about . . . were you there?
>
> Jacques: Yes. It made the October crisis look like an incident in an alley. (191)

Since Binoy is a writer and an angry young man at that he makes certain remarks about the publication business. He remarks:

> No matter what you say about the British, they're not [fucking] shallow. . . . In fact, I was just telling Neela the other day . . . that I would like it if the book got published in England . . . and she said a group of publishers there are looking for new works by Indian writers that could be sold and the money would be sent to Bhopal. (235)

There is also an incidental criticism of American publishing. He remarks that to be accepted by an American publisher if he "could add something like the Maharani of Jaipur was financing the contras with hash . . . from Iran, while her granddaughter was having a steady romance in Honduras with a contra leader . . . something like that would sell." (234) There are many parodies which are hilarious. In fact, the very first appearance of Baba Jacques is hilarious: "Jacques appears from a tunnel of light. Long hair, big beard with a bad toothy smile. Muttering a sloka. (Om Mani Padme Om)" (188)

The play *Baba Jacques* has everything to make it a success on the stage. It has even very interesting visual effects that have been worked into the stage directions including an element of the appearance of the ghosts because after all a part of the play takes place in a cemetery where Baba Jacques lives with the ghosts. Scene II of the play is placed in the cemetery. The stage direction reads:

> The night outline of Montreal, Mountain with cross. Scene in Cote-des-Neiges cemetery. Shaft of light at a raised level. Bell music. Very dark dim lighting. Like a blue haze. Mysterious. In the background . . . vaults lying side by side with numbers on them. Some tombstones in the background. (185)

There is a certain atmosphere which is surrealistic though it is handled in eerie comic context. "Neela goes over to vault 49 and opens it. An ashen faced woman in a long white gown steps out. Lights dim elsewhere." (182) The following stage direction makes the point quite clear:

> Noise of knocking comes from one of the vaults. Whispered voice: "Hey! You open the latch here . . . hey you, here number 38, here, hurry up." . . . Neela walks closer, puts her ears to 38, hears the whisper again: "Here, open it, open it." As soon as Neela opens a wiry looking white man with a moustache and black frame glasses-leaps out yelling: "Free, free, free at last, Lord . . . free at last . . . On his knees." (197)

There are ghosts galore! There is an incredible combination of levity and seriousness in the play as it discusses the immigration policy of Canada on the one hand and the misunderstanding if not total lack of knowledge about India on the part of the Canadians. For example:

Esther: Do you have sex (she giggles) like in the Kam Soot?
Binoy: Not Kam Soot, ma'am, Kama Sutra. (193)

Rana Bose shares some of the anger of the Montreal rebel playwright Michel Tremblay when he says "Jan, my story is not about the gentle folks who live in Dollard-des Ormeauz or Laval on the Lake." (178) In the same way, Tremblay talks about Outremont section of Montreal. Indeed, Bose actually mentions Tremblay at one point in the play when he makes Binoy say:

> What is self-indulgence? Can you imagine and he's not even your regular Canadian writer with a name like Tremblay or McPherson. And how obscure can the subject be? I mean who cares about growing up in Montreal with Indian parents, who don't want to have nothing to do with their past or the present for that matter, except some vague shit about retaining one's heritage and culture. (208)

There is a reference to writers like Paul Scott and Bharati Mukherjee as the protagonist of the play happens to be a writer. About Baba Jacques, a number of details about his association with India emerge in the course of the play. For example:

Hostess: I thought he was a hippy.
MA: Yes, all the hippies who remained hippy are dangerous.
Hostess: What do you mean?
MA: He went to India in 1972—you know, these (walking a little) misguided youth of the west—smoking marijuana in Kathmandu and lying naked on the beach in Goa.
Hostess: Not Merrijana—marihuana . . . bahen.
MA: Yes, they also call it grass . . . but anyway—grass, weed, whatever he had—I heard India had a profound effect on him . . . he felt Western youth were ignoring India's poor and romanticizing philosophy and culture and past. (229)

Whatever the opinion of Binoy in the play or of the author Rana Bose, the present writer would like to say that he has himself personally met many of the hippies in Goa in the 60s and 70s and found some of them extraordinarily intelligent, well-read and well-informed people who were simply rebelling against the restrictions against their personal freedom in the West. Thus, he has sympathy for Baba Jacques, however freaky and strange he may seem to be. Like John Osborne's Jimmy Porter, Binoy of Rana Bose attacks everything under the sun, including Montreal the city of his choice when he makes a parody of the television reporter:

> Nick recounts saying good morning to him, while a deranged looking man with curly hair was seen prowling around at the back towards Dorchester. Station 25 policeman James D'arcy later said that they had put together a composite and were on the lookout for a man from the St. Henri district who was known to be prowling the Crescent Bishop neighbourhood in the early hours of the morning. . . . (Turns to the audience) It's here, folks. In the heart of our city in Downtown Montreal. Like an epidemic, like you've never seen it before, an alien spirit has descended on our fair city . . . and I tell ya—this city is turning the way of Toronto . . . growing levels of unscrupulous immigration have led to acute job shortages. . . . Youth from St. Henri and Cote des Neiges districts are prowling in the downtown subways. . . . Restless, jobless and with only their blasters to comfort them. . . . Montreal is shaping up for a hot summer. (201)

In this play, there is incidental negative references to the city of Toronto. At one point in the play we are told that Binoy is beaten up in Toronto. Scene IV of the play is placed in the Subway at Toronto and "Binoy gets violently beaten up. Subway train roars by with lighting effect." (210) We get to know more about Toronto in Bose's play *Five or Six Characters in Search of Toronto*. However, any further comment on Toronto is outside the scope of the present essay. Uma Parameswaran points out: "Each of Bose's plays is a delight to read. In *Baba Jacques*, there is a sheer exuberance of imagination; the French Canadian mystic lives in the cemetery, and a stage full of characters-journalist Matt, Esther Crawford whose family owns a brewery and publishing house, bigoted Mr. Fraser—walk in and out of their vaults; the structure and stylistic techniques of the play are influenced by classical tradition and contemporary experimentation; the central thrust of the play is definitely a satirical look at South Asians' view of life in Canada and other Canadians' view of South Asians in Canada." (xvii)

In approaching South Asian Canadian theatre, one needs to understand two historical Indian bases to the theatre of protest developed by South Asian Canadians. One, this genre owes its format to the people's theatre movement in Bengal led by Badal Sircar, and the Marxist movement in India in the earlier decades of this century. Two, it uses many of the standard stage techniques and strategies used by folk theatre in India over the centuries. Thus, we must remember that while the plots move around the problems faced by South Asians and other "visible minorities" in Canada, many of the stage techniques are a transplant from India's folk and popular traditions. (v)

NOTES

1. Hugh MacLennan, *The Watch that Ends the Night* (Toronto: Macmillan of Canada, 1958), p. 255.
2. Rana Bose, "Baba Jacques Dass and Turmoil at Cote-Des-Neiges Cemetery," *Saclit Drama Plays by South Asian Canadians*, ed. Uma Parameswaran (IBH, 1996), pp. 174-242.
3. A.M. Klein, ed., "Montreal," *The Oxford Book of Canadian Verse in English and French* (Toronto: Oxford University Press, 1965), pp. 260-61.

"Home is Where Our Feet Are": A Diasporic Study of Stephen Gill's *Immigrant*

D. PARAMESWARI
Madurai-Kamaraj University

The term 'diaspora' literally refers to man's scattering in an alien soil, far away from homeland. It implies a cultural travel, a nostalgic reminiscence of home—the culture of origin and an anchoring in the new world—the culture of adoption. While analyzing the problems of the Indian diaspora in Canada, Uma Parameswaran writes "Home is where our feet are and we had better place our heart where the feet are."[1] The man who settles abroad as an immigrant finds a location even as he remains an exile suffering from inevitable isolation. Then which is his home?—the new land of which he has dreams or the one he has left behind?

The theme of home/homelessness is an age-old issue pressing the minds of the indigenous population and the settlers, ever since man started travelling from place to place. One of the trio in Indian English writing, Raja Rao once said "I carry India with me wherever I go." Living away from Ireland, James Joyce wrote only about his native land, his "dear, dirty Dublin." Katherine Mansfield, settled in England, declared "Wherever I live I write with New Zealand in my bones."[2] The Poland-born Conrad, having left his country while it was struggling for freedom from the Russian rule, wrote volumes of essays and novels on every topic other than the slavery and the independence of his country and subsequently suffered lifelong an acute sense of guilt. For all immigrants, intense nostalgia is an inevitable outcome of their displacement.

With regard to the Indians settled in Canada, the problem of isolation and fear may not be as complex as it is for the ones who move to Canada for professional and educational requirements. Of the latter category, "some never grow past the phase of nostalgia. Romanticizing one's own native land has a place, so long as it does not paralyze one's adopted homeland. Nostalgia as the only sustenance can become quite toxic, vitiating the living stream into a stagnant cesspool."[3] The former category, probably the youngsters, are more flexible, being able to synthesize the old and the new.

Stephen Gill's second novel *Immigrant* waxes eloquent over the trials and tribulations of an Indian immigrant in Canada. Reghu Nath's existence in Canada signals a shunting between a wilful regression to India and a forced progression towards Canada. "Gill creates a text and a context to cope with the politics of sharing and survival, the communication problems and socio-economic and political contradictions, ambiguities and racist and ethnic prejudices that cause disillusionment and distrust in an immigrant in everyday life."[4]

As the novel opens, the young Reghu Nath from India is flying over the Atlantic and his flight landing late by seven hours causes him anxiety and he enters Montreal when Canada is busy with its centennial celebration, Expo '67. Accommodation poses problems and Reghu must reach Ottawa "at least three days before" in order to register himself for admission to a Ph.D. programme in the University. In an alien soil, he is restless and disturbed, with not a soul to help him. The rigid, demanding and prejudiced professors at the University, the unfamiliar Canadian accent and the register of the English language spoken, the confusing grading system, the adamant Canadian bureaucracy and the stubbornly haunting memories of India are the troubleshooters to Reghu Nath: "within a week Reghu found himself surrounded by many different problems. Financially, his position was not sound, educationally he did not know where he headed. Psychologically, he was yet not adjusted to his new environment." At the university, he found himself open to the whims of his instructors and accepted what they asked of him. As far as social life was concerned, it was almost non-existent. The professors and students used to come to class on time, then disperse mechanically soon after the class was over."[5] He finds the Canadian women totally uncompromising and difficult. "He mustered all his courage to say politely 'I love you.' The girl glanced to one side, then the other, before finishing her whisky in a gulp." (18) New words, unintelligible expressions and slang take him unawares.

Reghu next experiences culture-shocks, the ones that he could least digest. While shopping, he holds the hand of a compatriot from India, the man instantaneously severs his hand and retorts: "This is not India." Surprised by his curt behaviour Reghu demands, "What do you mean?" The man casually replies "Don't you know it yet?" Reghu pleads ignorance: "There are many things for me to know." The man explains "people will think we are homos." Not knowing the real meaning of the short word 'homo,' Reghu becomes quiet and then clarifies: "Do you mean homosexuals?" The friend confirms in turn. After this incident, he keenly observes others but never finds a man holding hands with another man.

Next, Reghu meets Mrs. Wallace, a pseudo freelancer-cum-frustrated artist, living next to Reghu's. "At the age of sixty she was more interested in sex than in money. The unemployed boy whom Reghu runs into tells him that "he was a handyman for Mrs. Wallace and received $15 every time he rendered her personal service at night." (40) Another neighbour who lives in a high-rise complex down the street from his room, a musician who plays a blues song on his guitar, during a courtesy visit, pulls out an empty beer bottle from under the bed and asks him to return it and buy a beer for him. When Reghu resists, with a pain in his voice, the man shrieks: "Why don't you go now and leave me alone." (41) A resident of the building in which he lives thunders amidst an argument, "why don't you go back to your country?" (42) "You should go back to India and leave us alone, too." (22) The white girls expect "to be treated as special, almost as China dolls, and disliked being touched in any way on the first date." They contend, "a woman has to be emotionally involved with a man before she gives herself to him." (24)

The idealist Reghu is not able to cope with the corrupt practices in his educational institution. He quits the university without obtaining his degree. He also realizes that Canada does not need scholars or people specialized in one branch or field." (25) "Canada had a handful of openings, usually filled by persons born here or by British and American immigrants, who encountered no prejudice because they were not a visible minority like the Africans and the Asians who spoke differently and looked differently." (25) Due to Canada's discriminatory policy the Indian Prabha, graduates in Library Science, but was forced to do cataloguing, though persons with less education and experience are given better positions, is driven to commit suicide. The Ph.D.s who have given almost half of their lives to learning and whose Indian parents anxiously look forward to the day when their children would hold responsible positions in Canada and bring credit to the family, end up "rusting, just stinking." (111) Dr. Hafeez, a renowned scientist from Bangla Desh, with his extensive research in liquid fuel combustion is forced to accept the offer as laboratory assistant, despite his established reputation in the U.K. Another Ph.D. in Political Science, Reghu reads in a newspaper, after a number of years of University teaching in India, finds himself jobless in Canada and at last becomes a waiter in a Toronto restaurant.

Ethnic and racial prejudices and biases grow in leaps and bounds day by day. "An Asian immigrant is slapped and pushed by white boys from Toronto station platform onto the subway track" (116), "the victim spent four and a half months in hospital, and eight months in bed. He lost both legs." (117) "The matter was dismissed by the Police." (117) Further, the immigration officials strategically discouraged the Asians from coming to Canada. In Ottawa a children's Aid Society discourages adoption of white children by Asians. Many school councillors in the Toronto area do not permit the Asian children to select certain subjects for study. "An Asian in Toronto was harassed by a child. Angry, the Asian hit the child slightly. Someone reported it to the police and the Asian was fined 200 dollars." (120) In another incident, though a whiteman bumps a car from behind and admits his mistake, the police gives tickets to both. Racial assault is widely prevalent. "In Brampton, a Tanzanian, mistaken for a Pakistani, had his house painted by racial slogans by five boys. Later, thèy were arrested and punished by the judge who ordered him to write an essay on Pakistan. They were also ordered by the judge to spend an evening with the family of the Canada-Pakistan-Associations President which included a spicy meal." (118)

The Canadian government disgraces welfare recipients like Reghu. The manpower office is silent or indifferent. There is an unending conflict between the white and the settlers. "Many white Canadians blamed immigrants, particularly the visible minority, for their unemployment. They said that the immigrants had taken jobs from them and that they were accepting any work on far below the minimum wage set up by the government." (115) They accepted jobs in a pinch and quit as soon as they qualified for themselves for unemployment. The white employees were extremely satisfied with the studious nature of the immigrant workers who, they said, "were prepared to work after service hours and on weekends." A sense of jealousy and a climate of uncertainty widen the gulf between the white Canadians and the newcomers, particularly from the regions of India, Pakistan, Bangladesh and Sri Lanka.

Though placed in the midst of struggle, Reghu is not prepared to advocate any malicious notion, vindictive attitude, or egoistic response. He gradually understands that if the immigrants suffer harassment and violence, it is not because of the fellow Canadian citizens. It is the people with power who spread the venom of discrimination. "Obviously, it was a tactic of the ruling power to divert the citizen's attention from the country's growing economic unrest." (134) With such a seed of maturity sprouting in his mind, Reghu, at the end, realizes "The whole world is my country. I am a world citizen." (142) It is here that Reghu tells himself: "I don't see any difference. Men and women all over the world are the same basically. These so-called cultures are man-made and cause anarchy and confusion." (66)

Reghu willingly rejects what had become part of him (India) in order to adapt the values of the new land (Canada).

Reghu's merger with the Canadian culture is symptomatic of his newfound knowledge that "Home is where the feet are, and we had better place our heart where the feet are." (39) His home now moves from India to Canada, the wheat-granary of the world which at last comes forward to feed this one Indian also.

Thus, the remedial strategy which Stephen Gill recommends to a fellow immigrant is integration with the white majority, an ideology advocated by another marginalized poet, Countee Cullen from the Harlem Renaissance Movement, to his brethren in the black community.

NOTES

1. Uma Parameswaran, "Home is Where Your Feet are, and May Your Heart be There too," *Writers of Indian Diaspora: Theory and Practice,* ed. Jasbir Jain (New Delhi: Rawat, 1998), p. 30.
2. Anisur Rahman, *New Literatures in English* (New Delhi: Creative, 1991), p. xiv.
3. Parameswaran, p. 32.
4. R.K. Singh "Cross Cultural Communication," *Language Forum,* Vol. XXIV, No. 1-2, Jan.-Dec. 1998, p. 81.
5. Stephen Gill, *Immigrant* (Ontario: Vesta, 1982), pp. 15-16.

"Two Cupboards": Transcultural Discourse in Rohinton Mistry's Short Stories

CHARU C. MISHRA
K.G. Arts and Science College, Raigarh

In an interview with Linda Hutcheon, this is how Rohinton Mistry voiced his opinion about the clash between the old culture of India and the new culture of Canada in his works: "If you have a cupboard with a certain amount of space in it, then you have to arrange your belongings in that cupboard the best way you can, given the space. But if you buy a new cupboard you have more space."[1] Undoubtedly, by referring to the two cupboards, Mistry makes his intention clear about the presentation of transcultural space in his fiction. Like most of his contemporary Canadian writers of South Asian origin, Mistry too can boast of a double identity: Indian by birth and Canadian by present habitation. In addition to his proximity to Indian culture, he hails from the Parsi community that has undergone double diaspora, first from Persia to India (Sanjan in Gujarat) after Arabic invasion in 7th century A.D. and second from there to other parts of India especially Bombay in the later stages. Personally Mistry authenticates another diaspora by virtue of his immigration to Canada. Undeniably Mistry has acquired enough experience that need arrangement in his two cupboards.

Mistry's present place of habitation, a nation with "too much geography" and "no particular history?" poses a challenge to all immigrants.[2] It is the challenge of charting a "cultural territory"[3] of one's own or be doomed with a hyphenated identity forever. Mistry has not only accepted this challenge but has also been able to carve out a niche for himself in the arena of Canadian literature through his fictional discourse. By situating his story scapes in the locale of both the nations, he has founded an ideal space where greying of the two nations has been achieved artistically.

In this paper I propose to study the juxtaposition of inter cultural space of India and Canada in two of Mistry's short stories "Squatter" and "The Swimming Lessons" and show how he has arranged the space of the two metaphorical cupboards simultaneously weaving the double vision of immigrants into their themes.

In "Squatter," the cultural space of two apparently diverse nations, India and Canada, are brought together through immigration of a Parsi youngman, Sarosh, to Toronto. Before his departure a farewell party was arranged for him where he gets mixed response from his friends and relatives regarding his decision. While some said that "his whole life would change for the better"; others said "immigration was all wrong, but if he wanted to be unhappy that was his business, they wished him well."[4] To silence their debate he makes a casual announcement before all of them: "If I don't become completely Canadian in exactly ten years from the time I land there, then I will come back." (154-55)

It is around this problematic that Mistry's transcultural discourse revolves, Sarosh's adaptation to the new country would have been complete had it not been for so trivial a problem like his failure at using the WC. He remains dependent on the old way of squatting to relieve himself. Sarosh who now calls himself Sid finds his casual announcement hanging over him "with the awesome presence and sharpness of a guillotine." (154) The conflicting space of the two nations is signified by the veritable world of washroom where Misty brings out the clash of culture effectively:

> The world of washroom is private at the same time very public. The absence of feet below the stall door, the smell of faeces, the rustle of paper, glimpses caught through the narrow crack between stall door and jamb all these added upto only one thing: a foreign presence in the stall, not doing things in the conventional way. And if the one outside could receive the fetor of Sarosh's business waiting through the door, poor unhappy Sarosh too could detect

> something malodorous in the air: the presence of xenophobia and hostility. (156)

Through such humorous exposure, Mistry does not aim to slight Sarosh's predicament, on the contrary it is his typical way of showing the double vision of immigrants. Deep inside him, he feels a nostalgic yearning for the left behind culture that shaped his habits like squatting on the toilet. While outside in his present state, he attempts to place himself in the new culture, simultaneously preserving his differentness. Sarosh's subsequent meeting with Mrs. Maha-lepate in the office of the Immigration Aid society exposes him to this fact. Canada happens to be a nation of wonderbread, that induces vomiting in some Indians, its water undrinkable for a Sri Lanka woman and a whole Pakistani family "chock on their own saliva" (158-59) as they can not swallow. It seems as if a miniscule Asia when brought to the threshold of Canadian culture finds it too repulsive.

Canadian multiculturalism which is the official policy of the government to encourage peaceful co-existence of diverse race and culture comes under severe criticism of Nariman Hansotia, the storyteller of Ferozsha Baag:

> The multicultural Department is a Canadian invention. It is supposed to ensure that ethnic cultures are able to flourish, so that Canadian society will consist of mosaic of cultures that's their favorite word, mosaic instead of one uniform mix, like the American melting pot. If you ask me, mosaic and melting pot are both nonsense, and ethnic is a polite way of saying bloody foreigner. (160)

Quite skilfully, Mistry brings forward the debate surrounding multiculturalism that has held the nation's intellectuals and academics for more than three decades now. There is a growing feeling now that this linguistically neutral and politically correct term has not been able to solve all the problems surrounding the ethnic minority and achieve cultural balance as issues like subtle racism are still there to be dealt with effectively.[5]

The suggestion of Dr. No-Ilaaz to implant a Crappus Non-Interruptus (CNI) with financial assistance from Multicultural Department in Sarosh's body too slights the activities of the multicultural Department. In any case, Sarosh rejects this suggestion which would enable him to evacuate himself like a machine. His maniac obsession with relieving himself in the western style and long stretches in the washroom cost him his job. Curiously, he is able to adapt himself in this, great little act in the washroom of the aeroplane which is taking him back to India. Ironically Canada the so-called land of milk and honey remains undiscovered due to "a pain in the posterior" (168) the pull of the old place, the India of squatters. However, his final adaptation, belated though, keeps alive the hope of greying in future.

In his story "The Swimming Lessons" Mistry brings the two nations closer to the point of cross-cultural communication. The contours of both the nations get properly outlined here. The earlier conflict of adaptation to the new land is over. The narrator protagonist Kersi from Ferozsha Baag who is the "fictional surrogate"[6] of the writer already lives in an apartment house in Don Mills, Toronto which also houses people of diverse races and culture. This diverse populace includes a Portuguese woman; an old man on wheel chair along with his divorced daughter from Vancouver; Bertha, her husband and son from Yugoslavia; two white women whose nationalism is not clear. It seems Mistry has deliberately located his storyscape in the multicultural Canada to bring out the race relation to the forefront.

In Don Mills's apartment block, the inter-personal communication among the residents is almost rare. The Portuguese woman is the only connecting thread that weaves the lives of all of them. Through her remarks, the readers become aware of their activities. The oldman always seen on his wheel chair in the lobby is also a cardiac patient and is taken care of by his divorced daughter. He is in the habit of putting a set question "How old do you think I am" (230) to every neighbour passing through the lobby which betrays his anxiety and loneliness. It brings out the parallel suffering and loneliness of the narrator hero's grandfather in Parsi General Hospital in Bombay. His failure to form an acquaintance with the man and share his life is only a reminder of his guilty conscience for not visiting his grandfather in the hospital during his last days as often. Mistry's arrangement of the spaces of the two cupboards, the contents from his past memory and present experience, can be clearly marked in such presentation.

Mistry's artistic merit in the portrayal of various characters with their unique behaviour helps him bring out the diversity of Canadian society effectively. Bertha, the building superintendent, is a big Yugoslavian woman who is very prompt in her job. Her husband who misses work most of the days due to his boozing and her son who tinkers with the van are obvious targets of her Slavic tirade. The Portuguese woman's attempt to get information about others by keeping her door open and sharing them through her short remarks with the narrator-hero too betrays her loneliness. While such behaviour from Bertha and the Portuguese woman must not be taken as characteristic of any race, they do point to the inherent differentness of the Canadian society.

Mistry's narrator-hero, while working as a clerk in the insurance company, enrolls himself for swimming lessons in the High School behind his apartment. The Chaupaty Beach near his house in Bombay is too dirty to arouse such passion in him. The disposal of coconuts and clay gods and goddesses by the Hindus, ashes of the sacred sandalwood fire and the leftovers of the deadmen by the Parsis in the sea reflects the Indian cultural practices and the squalid sea water contrasts the clear blue water of the high school swimming pool in Toronto. It is here that the narrator-hero must satisfy his urges for swimming and enliven his sexual fantasy aroused by the two white women of the third floor while sunbathing themselves in the patchy lawn of his apartment house. Even in his fantasy, Mistry does not forget to hint about a possible union of the two *races;* one from black India and the other from white Canada:

> a gorgeous woman m the class for non-swimmers at whose sight I will be instantly aroused, and she spying the shape of my desire, will look me straight in the eye with her intentions; she will come home with me, to taste the pleasures of my delectable Asian brown body whose strangeness has intrigued her and unleashed uncon-

> trollable surges of passion inside her throughout the duration of swimming lessons. (235-36)

However, before such a fantastic union could materialize, he must join the swimming lesson class which again consists of a group of mixed racial origin. Like the earlier story, the subtle hints of racism and xenophobia is again recounted by Mistry in the washroom of the swimming lesson class:

> As I enter the showers three young boys, probably from previous class, emerge. One of them holds his nose. The second begins to hum, under his breath: Paki, Paki, smell like curry. The third says to the first two: pretty soon all the water is going to taste of curry. (238)

Such sly comments under the breath point at the unavowed racism of Canadian multicultural society. Finally, the narrator-hero's swimming pool fantasy comes to an end when he finds himself at the verge of drowning, while volunteering for a demonstration. His final comments bring out the inner feelings of immigrants evocatively: "Maybe the swimming pool is the hang out of some racist group, bent on eliminating all non-white swimmers to keep their waters pure and their white sisters unogled." (239)

It is due to such countering of racism through sexist remarks that Mistry has earned the sharp criticism of Janette Turner Hospital: "In 'Swimming Lessons,' which charts most closely the cultural displacement of the young Parsi in Toronto, I was forcibly struck by the narrator's blind spot, an unintentional one, I suspect, on the author's part. The swimmer alludes (without comment and hence powerfully) to racist gestures and remarks made by other in the locker room; but he himself frequently makes extremely sexist observations about women and seems unaware of the parallel insult."[7]

While Mistry may be discounted for any such aberration in his fictional character, his higher motif of juxtaposing the culture of the two nations deserves our appreciation. Honestly enough he does not forget to expose the cultural conflicts and nuances of his erstwhile nation. The echoes of Maharashtra for Maharashtrians carries with it the racism and growing influence of the cultural major. The frequently striking and 'bundh' calling workers display the growing indiscipline and corruption rampant in post-Independence Indian society.

Mistry's narrator-hero is again and again glued to the wash room and water. As he himself says, "water imagery is recurring in my life: Chaupaty beach, swimming pool, and bathtub."[8] The squalid sea beach of Bombay is as much repulsive as the swimming pool of Toronto stinking of racism. After all these experiences of "the overwater world of washroom," he must plunge inside and search for new ones: "The world outside the water I have seen a lot of, it is now time to see what is inside."[9]

His frequent reference to water imagery evidently brings us to the symbolic watery space of multiculturalism where different race and culture could immerse, especially the ones from India and Canada so that the immigrant's fear and host's racism is washed clean.

While explaining the role of the immigrant writer, Stella Sandahl writes: "He is the one who can convey experiences from different worlds, being himself part of different worlds. Complexity does not mean schizophrenia. We can and should contribute to the common culture still remain ourselves."[10]

Mistry's transcultural discourse contributes a lot to the mainstream of Canadian culture, at the same time remains distinctly individual. As Hope Cooke writes: "Mistry steps out of frame to comment on his artistic patterning of life's material, both past and future. He uses his Toronto apartment house to evoke Ferozsha Baag, implying that the violent break of his immigration has in someway been healed, made more of a circular process."[11]

With success of his narrator-hero as a writer, Mistry's artistic patterning of life's materials achieves perfection. The successful blending of his Indian and Canadian experience in these stories simultaneously illumines and illustrates his metaphorical reference to the two cupboards. The national recognition for Mistry's contribution to Canadian multiculturalism and literature has already brought greying of India and Canada to fruition.

"Constructive co-existence among culturally and racially diverse communities, seems bound to become a mandatory 21st century skill."[12] Both India and Canada have the advantage of long experience in managing multicultural society. Mistry's transcultural discourse, in this regard, is a pointer to racism, a malady afflicting both the culture needs immediate and effective treatment that would pave the way for further greying of both the nations in the 21st century.

NOTES

1. *"Other Solitudes": Canadian Multicultural Fictions*, ed. Linda Hutcheon and Marion Richmond (Toronto: Oxford Univ. Press, 1990).
2. E.D. Blodgett, "Space subject syntax," *Open Letter*, Ninth Series No. 9, Summer 1997, pp. 88-108.
3. Edward Said, *Cultural and Imperialism* (London: Chatto and Windus, 1993).
4. Rohinton Mistry, "Swimming Lessons," *Tales from Ferozsha Baag* (New York, Vintage International, 1997), p. 154.
5. W.M. Verhoven "How Hyphenated Can You Get?: A Critic of Pure Ethnicity," *Mosaic*, vol. 29, No. 3, Sept. 96.
6. Michiko Kakutani, "Tales From a Bombay Apartment Complex," *The New York Times*, February 3, 1989, p. 32.
7. Janette Turner Hospital, "Living in Toronto, Dreaming of Bombay," *Los Angeles Times Book Review*, March 5, 1989, p. 211.
8. *Ibid.*, p. 248.
9. *Ibid.*, p. 249.
10. M.G. Vassanji, "A Meeting of Streams" (Toronto: TSAR, 1985), pp. 133-38.
11. Hope Cooke, "Beehive in Bombay," *The New York Times Book Review*, March 5, 1989, p. 26.
12. "Multiculturalism in Canada," *The Challenge of Diversity*, Augie Fleras and Jean Leonard Elliot (Ontario: Nelson Canada, 1992), p. 269.

Bad Faith in Rohinton Mistry's "Lend Me Your Light"

SUBHASH CHANDRA
S.B.S. College, University of Delhi

Sartre's concept of Bad Faith occupies an important place in the existentialist paradigm of authenticity of self in the hostile, despairing and life-negating environment. Doomed to exercise freedom of choice, as Sartre sees it, the self has to choose between one course of action and another (even not choosing and remaining passive signifies a choice) and then face the consequences of the choice. But how authentic one is in choosing or not choosing a course of action is a moot point, for one may invent attenuating circumstances/factors for justifying one's action/inaction. This act of manufacturing justificatory reasons is termed as Bad Faith by Sartre. In the present paper, I intend to examine the operation of Bad Faith in Mistry's story "Lend Me Your light."

This story begins with Tagore's words from *Gitanjali*: "Your lights are all lit—lend me your light." These words of Tagore acquire a piquant poignancy in the context of the story which, when analyzed, reveals the need for Indians to remain rooted to their soil, help their fellow brethren who are oppressed, deprived and exploited, but are completely helpless and at the mercy of the powerful. Most of the expatriate writers suffer from a sense of guilt, which gets reflected in their stories because though all writing, to a certain extent, is a process of self-analysis and a search for answers, the expatriate writing is more so. The question: "Is it desirable to leave one's country?" therefore becomes a tangled puzzle, the unravelling of which involves anguish, nostalgia, and guilt for the writers and their characters.

The reason for leaving one's country is always clear enough: better prospects and opportunities in the land of the plenty. But what is not foreseen by the migrant is the blurring of the definition of his own identity that is the unavoidable outcome of the transplanting process. Also what is not realized is the inauthenticity that comes to mark the lives of the migrants. Salman Rushdie, while talking of Guntur Grass, pinpoints the turbulence and turmoil a migrant goes through when he says: "A full migrant suffers, traditionally, a triple disruption: he loses his place, he enters into an alien language, and he finds himself surrounded by beings whose social behaviour and codes are unlike and sometimes even offensive to his own. And this is what makes a migrant such a pathetic figure, because roots, languages and social norms have been three of the most important parts of the definition of what it is to be a human being." Rushdie goes on to say, "The migrant, denied all three, is obliged to find new ways of describing himself, new ways of being human." And in this process of acquiring a new self-definition, often confusion persists and Bad Faith is practised.

Reverting to Tagore's words, the less fortunate seem to be importuning their comparatively better off brethren not to leave them, because they need their help, their sympathy, their attention. The villagers, living in far-flung places are poor and exploited. They need the help of their educated fellow human beings to be taken out of the clutches of the oppressors. The writer highlights the moral failure of those who go away, using the technique of comparison and contrast and seems to empathize with Percy who chooses to stay on in India and work among and for the villagers, even at the risk to his own life. But before taking up this contrast in detail, let us consider the case of comparison.

Of the three friends, Jamshed, Percy and Kersi (the latter two are brothers), Jamshed and Kersi leave for America and Canada (Toronto) respectively. The motives for migration are obviously material prosperity, better prospects for jobs and career advancement. The prospect of migration is a celebratory occasion and, therefore, Kersi receives plenty of congratulatory greetings and blessings on the occasion of his departure. The narrator-protagonist records: "Then the neighbours began to arrive. Over the course of the last seven days they came to confer their blessings and good wishes upon me." (178) Najama's blessings condense the general feeling: "Lots and lots of years you must live, see lots of life, study lots, earn lots, make us all very proud of you." (180)

Jamshed's letter from America to Kersi, who is in Canada, dubs India a "dismal place" where "Nothing ever improves, just too much corruption" which is "all part of the *ghati* mentality" (*ghati* is an umbrella word for a person who is menial, low and all that is undesirable). Kersi wonders why Jamshed is so much full of "disdain and discontentment even when he was no longer living under those conditions." (181) It seems inexplicable. But it is not so. The text provides the answer. I will point to it a little later.

Interestingly, Kersi is irritated by Jamshed's condemnation of India. He tries to prove him wrong by becoming a member of the Parsi-club and visiting Parsi get-togethers. He wants to be a part of India by participating in all that is Indian in Canada. His letter to Jamshed does not share Jamshed's contempt for India. But has Kersi found all the answers to the questions that trouble him as an immigrant? Is he at peace with himself as Percy is in India, trying to light the dark homes of the poor in villages?

Kersi's visit to India does not solve his riddles. Having defended India against Jamshed's criticism, he too indulges in Bad Faith. His words in this context reveal the truth: "Bombay seemed dirtier than ever. I remembered what Jamshed had written in his letter, and how it had annoyed me, but now I couldn't help thinking he was right. Hostility and tension seemed to be perpetually present in buses, shops, trains." (187) Mistry wants to make it clear that both these characters are being inauthentic, because he juxtaposes the pair with Percy—an individual whose self possesses integrity and authenticity. He, too, is living in the same Indian environment which is found to be insufferable by Jamshed and Kersi. If anything, he is living in worse conditions, involving threat to his very life, because he is working in a village as a part of a group of young, enthusiastic persons, who help the credit-burdened poor farmers. But he does not make the hostile and uncomfortable conditions an excuse for leaving Bombay for a foreign country. On the contrary, he has, in the words of Tagore, decided to lend his light to the deprived whose houses are dark. So, the inhospitable conditions cannot be used as alibis, according to the norms set out in the text by the author. If one turns away from these conditions, it is because one does not choose to engage with the prevailing reality. One does not have the courage to confront the contrary. The element of escapism is unmistakable in the stance taken by Jamshed and Kersi. To be authentic extracts some price. Percy is prepared to pay it. Jamshed and Kersi are not. But then people like Jamshed and Kersi pay another kind of price for being inauthentic. Confusion and misery afflict them. Kersi's self-definition remains fuzzy. He waits for an epiphany. But there are no epiphanies at the quotidian level of existence. One has to search for the answers and the process of searching for the answers brings one face to face with the unsavoury, quite often. Jamshed also pays a kind of price. Why is he so pathologically angry with Bombay? Here is an example of his sizzling anger. He has accidentally met Kersi near the Flora Fountain during his visit to Bombay (Kersi also happens to have come). Pointing to the pavement stalls he fumes: "Terrible, isn't it, the way these buggers think they own the streets—don't even leave you enough room to walk. The police should drive them off, break up their bloody stalls, really." (190) He is angry with Bombay. In fact, he is angry with himself, because he suffers from guilt. This is the answer to the question raised above. His anger has a cause, but it is not outside of himself.

However, Percy is at peace with himself. The group, of which he is a part, arranges interest-free loans for the farmers in the form of seeds and fertilizers at cheaper prices from the cooperative they have formed. The exploitative system, entrenched in the village, feels threatened and commits violence. They kill Navjeet, one of the members of the group. Percy is shocked, shaken and afraid. But the shock and the fear pass.

When the whole gruesome incident is related to Jamshed by Percy's mother, Jamshed's response is along the expected lines: "I told you from the beginning all this was a waste of time and nothing would come of it, remember? Every time we met we would talk about it, and you used to make fun of me wanting to go abroad. But I still think the best thing for you is to move to the States. There is so much you could achieve there. There, if you are good at something you are appreciated, and you get ahead. Not like here, where everything is controlled by uncle-auntie, and . . ." (192)

However, Percy discards Jamshed's selfish wisdom. He is no longer afraid. He turns to his mother and says in a quiet voice: "Could we have dinner right away? I have to meet my friends at eight o'clock. To decide our next move in the village." (192) Mistry obviously puts Percy on a higher moral pedestal in the story in relation to the other two. His authenticity is valorized. Jamshed with his guilt and anger and Kersi with his dichotomies, ambiguities and resultant confusions and blurred self, waiting for an epiphany are marginal human beings, practising Bad Faith. Kersi makes his choice and is prepared to face the consequences which might involve losing his life. But he is prepared for it. He chooses to be an authentic individual.

Works Cited

Mistry, Rohinton. 1993. *Tales from Firozsha Baag*. New Delhi: Rupa.

Rushdie, Salman. 1991. *Imaginary Homelands*. New Delhi: Penguin.

Ecology and Identity Crisis in Rohinton Mistry's *A Fine Balance*

CHARU C. MISHRA
K.G. Arts and Science College, Raigarh

> These temple destroyers, these devotees of ravaging commercialism seem to have a perfect control for nature, and instead of lifting their eyes to God of the Mountains, lift them to mighty dollar.
>
> John Muir, Founder of Sierra Club, California (1892)

Ecological concerns have been the subject of literature since time immemorial. However, the ecological movement in the last few decades has gained considerable momentum and vigorously drawn the attention of the intellectuals, academics, writers and scientists to the grave issue of Man-Land (Nature) relationship. We have but one earth to live in. Naturally, therefore, any threat perception to its flora and fauna, to its biological and physical Nature, has become the central concern in the ecological writings ensuing therefrom. Such environmental crisis that challenges the Mother Earth and makes the Man-Nature relationship too fragile and endangered has acquired an existential dimension. As 'conscious' and 'sensitive' artists, the writers of this world have, time and again, raised their formidable voices of protest against the unmindful destruction of natural resources and the "Civilization's intrusion upon the pristine wilderness." They have written quite vividly and elaborately about Man's relationship with Nature and the factors which are responsible to disrupt it and create existential problem.

Both the English and Canadian writers have responded to the ecological relationship between Man and the Nature around them differently. The Canadian encounters with the land otherwise termed 'Canadian Collision' reverses the traditional British portrayal of an embalmed and ennobling nature. John Moss terms it 'garrison mentality' and attributes the reason to the 'fragile' and 'precarious' state of a man balanced against the vast and hostile North-American environment. D.G. Jones maintains that the difference of outlook and treatment between the English and French Canadian writers is conditioned by their respective cultural and historical development and writes: "Compared to their English Canadian counterparts, many French Canadian writers have themselves been more deeply infected by the garrison mentality and that mentality has been reinforced by the weapons of western culture that French Canada has traditionally emphasized for use against a hostile world, namely, the spiritual weapons of detachment, of modification and renunciation. English-Canadian culture has generally placed more emphasis on the material weapons for transforming the world, on technology and scientific technique."[1] Both the English and French Canadian literature tends to be sterile due to their extremity of attitude and have been criticized by writers like Leonard Cohen in his *Beautiful Losers.*

In comparison to their English and French counterparts, the South Asian Canadian writers have treated man-nature relationship in their works from a completely different perspective. Particularly, for these writers hailing from a warm country like India, Nature in the mountainous region is considered to be more human-friendly than in the arid and desert region. As such, Eastern attitude toward Nature is based more on caring and sharing. But the influence of the western culture, especially their emphasis on technology and development, has become the chief cause for the environmental degradation and ecological crisis in a country like India. Such ecological crisis in the South-Asian countries demands an altogether different approach with a view to deal with the destructive effect of modernization based on consumerism and industrialization and the consequent existential crisis. Among the current brood of South Asian writers in Canada, Rohinton Mistry has dealt elaborately with this aspect of ecological and environmental crisis in his fiction.

In his novel *A Fine Balance,*[2] Mistry has portrayed a few characters' relationship with the Nature around them with utmost sensitivity and depth. Most of these characters belong to his own Parsi community, which is an ethnic minority in a predominantly Hindu India. Thus the existential crisis which they confront in their personal, social and national life constitutes the central concern of the novel. The protagonist Farokh Kohlah happens to be a victim of History, namely, the partition of India in 1947, a ruthless and selfish imposition of the British Colonizer: "A foreigner drew a magic line on a map and called it the new border; it became a river of blood upon the earth. And the orchards, fields, factories, businesses, all on the wrong side of that line, vanished with a wave of the pale conjuror's wand." (205)

Despite the loss of the vast family fortune, Farokh along with his wife Aban and little son Maneck continue to relish their life in the foot hills of the Northern mountain in India meeting out their needs from the small left out general store. In addition to this Farokh had been handed over a secret soft drink formula by his father, popular as Kaycey and quite a rage among the small town people. Though his wife's people living in a city by the sea beseeched them periodically to leave the mountain and move over to their place, Farokh and his family continue to live in their home in the hills praising always, "The air and water is so pure, the mountains so beautiful." Like his father, son Maneck too loves his home in the mountain to such an extent that his temporary departure for the city for education makes him nostalgic. Even a steaming bowl of water in the bathroom brings to his mind the vision of the dreamy mist that would be hugging the mountains in the morning:

> at this hour it would be swirling fancifully, encircling the snow-covered peaks. Just after dawn was the best time to observe the slow dance, before the sun was strong enough to snatch away the veil. And he would stand at the window, watch the pink and orange of sunrise, imagine the mist tickling the mountain's ear chucking it under the chin or weaving a cap for it. (201)

Though Farokh had lost one of his eyes in an accident while bottling Kohlah's Cola and wore an eyepatch on it, on his long evening walks through the hillside forest he would put it in his pocket and admire for the umpteenth time the beauty of the place. His wife Aban too enjoyed the magnificent view of the valley from the back of the general store. Not only for Farokh and his family, but for his friends like Major Grewal and others also the mountain was a part of their life like a living intimate persona as if they lived together side by side. However their harmonious relationship with the nature was soon disrupted by the government's plan to connect the hill town to the cities. They who never dreamt of leaving the mountain were shocked to find the mountain leaving them. Mistry's subtle and veiled criticism is candid enough to target the self-styled messiahs for the development of the nation:

> These were to be modern roads . . . roads that would hum with the swift passage of modern traffic. Roads wide and heavy duty, to replace the scenic mountain paths too narrow for the broad vision of nation builders and World Bank officials. (215)

Threatened by the forces of modernization and urbanization which would eventually destroy the green mountain and the environment of the hill-town, Farokh and his friend Major Grewal organize meetings to condemn "the flawed development policy, the shortsightedness, the greed that was sacrificing the country's natural beauty to the demon of progress." (215) They sign petition and lodge their protest with the authorities, and wait. To their utter dismay, the authorities, those messengers of development equipped with the western ideas of technology and urbanization turn a deaf ear to their fervent appeal. The road continues to inch upwards, swallowing everything on its path. The invasion of technology is presented by Mistry quite evocatively:

> The beautiful hills by its side become gashed and scarred. From high on the slopes, the advancing tracks looked like rivers of mud defying gravity as though nature had gone mad. The distant thunder of blasting and the roar of earth-moving machines floated up early in the morning and the dreaminess of the dawn mist turned to nightmare.

More than anybody else Farokh Kohlah is shocked to the core of his heart. He feels as if he has been displaced from his dear land once again. The devastation of nature around him makes him depressed and terrified. His mental state is captured in the following touching lines:

> Mr. Kohlah watched helplessly as the asphalting began, changing the brown rivers into black, completing the transmogrification of his beloved birthplace where his forefathers had lived as in paradise. He watched powerlessly, while, for the second time, lines on paper ruined the Kohlah family. Only this time, it was an indigenous surveyor's cartogram, not a foreigner's imperial map. (216)

Ironically enough, the nation's plan primarily deprives him of his family fortune but holds out the promises of increased business in the second place. But in its promises lurks the venom of modernization which would deprive him of the family's name and his sense of identity. He complains to his wife bitterly that "the noxious exhaust from the lorries was searing his nostrils and the ugly throbbing of their engines was ripping his eardrums to shreds." Along with the pollution of air and noise, which is the primary cause of ecological imbalance, the so-called modernization brings in hordes of job-seekers who live in shacks and shanties by the slope of the hill and defile the environment through defecation and devour the forest for firewood. Farokh is shocked by a permanent stench of human waste that hung in the mountain air and to see "bold patches upon the body of the hill." As though corresponding to the protagonist's feelings of convulsion and anguish, the nature too reacts sharply against the technological invasion unleashed upon it, as Mistry notes:

> Then the seasons revolted. The rain which used to make things grow and ripen descended torrentially on the denuded hills, causing mudslides and avalanches. Snow, which had provided an ample blanket for the hills, turned skimpy. Even at the height of winter the cover was ragged and patchy. (217)

Farokh felt a perverse satisfaction at nature's rebellion. It was a vindication of sorts: he was not alone in being appalled by the hideous rape of the environment. But the seasonal disorder continued year after year only to break him deep down inside. Taking a walk in the hills, the long solitary rambles which were the greatest pleasure to invigorate him, now seemed like a death-watch. Haunted by the continual loss of the trees and rocks of the dearest mountain where he belonged, Farokh desperately looks for them:

> Coming upon a favorite tree, he would stop under its branches a while before moving on. He would run his hand along the gnarled trunk, happy that an old friend had survived another day. (217-18)

The menace of modernization causes ecological imbalance and consequently, an existential dilemma for Farokh. While the people's comments about the disillusioned protagonist, "Mr. Kohllah's screw is getting a little loose. He speaks to trees and rocks and pats them like they were his dogs," bring out his mental state, it also impress upon us his desperate search for his old place in the lap of nature. At this juncture, Mistry's portrayal of the protagonist is that of a knowledgeable, sensitive and spiritual person based upon idealism and traditionalism, while the generation of people around him stand out in stark contrast as ignorant, insensitive and materialists charged with spirit of modernization and change.

Finally, it was a heart-rending vision of the sunset during his walk in the hillside that conveys Farokh the inevitable message he was so desperately waiting for:

> Suddenly he noticed that dusk had fallen: the sunset was forfeited behind the pall. And the entire scene was so mean and squalid by the twilight, so utterly beyond his ability to accept or comprehend. He felt lost and frightened. Waves of anger, compassion, disgust, sorrow, failure, betrayal, love surged and crashed, battering and confusing him. For what? Of whom? And why was it? If only he could. (218)

Unable to make out the myriads of confusing emotions, Farokh feels a tightness in his chest, then his throat constricts as if he were choking. He weeps helplessly, silently venting his emotions. The meaning that this vision gives him is too new and terrifying for him to explore. There is no place for escape and he realizes that "his dreams had succumbed, during their collision with the passing years. He had struggled, he had won, he had lost. He would keep on struggling." (219)

A further bout of displacement catches him unaware, through modern material force of consumerism. Their technique of 'hard-sell' and cut-throat competition targets to overtake the sale of his family soft drink, Kaycey forcing it to the brink of closedown. Though his son Maneck, being modern generation young man, welcomes the idea of change and improvement in the general store, Farokh looks for his identity in the restoration of the past. He has an honest and touching reply about the consumerist culture and its garbed language like 'hard-sell':

> What kind of a language is that? Sounds absolutely undignified. Like begging. Those big companies from the city can behave like barbarians if they want to. Here we are civilized people. (220)

The modern generation has no place for such traditional and old-fashioned men and no honour for their sentiment. By his resistance to modernization and change, Farokh loses both his son and his own place in the scheme of a transmogrified homeland.

The final wish of Farokh after his death speaks volumes about the intense shock and anguish he had undergone by the invasion of modernization and its accompanying forces like consumerism and technology. Disillusioned by the way his dearest home-land in the hills was devastated and defiled, he wishes to be cremated and to get his ashes scattered in all the difficult places and terrains of his dear hills. Primarily, his wish for cremation was an outraging one as his religion Zoroastrianism prescribes the disposal of dead body by feeding it to vultures. Anticipating that any left out part of his body might further defile the land, he even dares to violate the sanction of his religion. Furthermore, by the consummation of his final wish with scattering of his ashes over the hills and the valley, Farokh seeks his lost identity through complete assimilation with his dearest trees, rocks and hills.

Man interacts with nature through the medium of culture. It is culture which provides the values and knowledge for man-land (Nature) interaction. Mistry's message in this regard is quite candid and radical. As long as the cultural values are sensitive to ecology, man's relationship with Nature remains harmonious and cordial. But when we adopt cultural values alien and unsuitable to our environment lured by its superficial and glamorous facade, a vicious circle of destruction and decay is unleashed, whose swift currents wash down the life-sustaining elements of nature. "Modernization and development through technology and science," a concept of the western culture is not an unwelcome idea. Rather, Mistry seems to suggest that its mindless execution without proper introspection and planning would adversely affect Nature, thereby creating ecological and existential crisis. Through his elaborate and sensitive presentation of man-nature relationship. Rohinton Misty stands out as another spokesman of ecological movement.

NOTES

1. D.G. Jones, "Butterfly in the Rock" (Toronto: Univ. of Toronto Press, 1970), p. 9.
2. Rohinton Mistry, *A Fine Balance* (London: Faber and Faber, 1996).

Ties and Trials in Rohinton Mistry's *Family Matters*

PARMANAND JHA
C.M. College, Darbhanga

Rohinton Mistry is a widely acclaimed writer of Indian English fiction. Born into a Parsi family in Bombay in 1952, Mistry studied Mathematics before he immigrated with his wife, an English teacher, to Toronto (Canada) in 1975. Even as he had no definite plan to be a writer, he began writing stories in 1983, while doing the job of a bank clerk by day and attending night courses at the University of Toronto. His attempts at short stories won him two Hart House Literary prizes and Canadian Fiction Magazine's Annual Contributor's Prize for 1985. In 1987 Penguin Books Canada published his *Tales from Firozsha Baag*, a collection of 11 short stories. Four years later, in 1991, Mistry published his first novel *Such a Long Journey*. It won him the Governor General's Award, the Commonwealth Writer's Prize for the best book and the Smith Books in Canada First Novel award and was shortlisted for the Booker Prize as well as for the Trillium Award. It has been translated into German, Swedish, Norwegian, Danish and Japanese. His second novel, *A Fine Balance*, published in 1995, won the prestigious Giller Prize, the Commonwealth Writer's Prize for the best book, the Los Angeles Times Book Prize for Fiction and the Royal Society of Literature's Winfred Hotby Award. It was also shortlisted for the Booker Prize, the International IMPAC Dublin Literary Award and the Irish Times International Fiction Prize. It was recently chosen as the first Canadian Pick for Oprah Winfrey's Book Club. *Family Matters* is Mistry's latest novel, shortlisted again, for Booker Prize.

Mistry has been described as a genius by a leading British newspaper[1] and a " true literary Map Maker."[2] His writing, he often admits, is the outcome of his passion for reading a variety of great authors from Enid Blyton to Chekhov, Joyce, Bellow, Updike and Naipaul. Living in Toronto for the last 27 years, Mistry has remained deeply rooted to his native place India. All his four books are set in Bombay that he "recreates and agonizes over with the close attention to detail of a homesick exile."[3] His novels are skilfully textured and compassionate stories of his native India and offer a genuine relief from the spicy, exotic 'Mango-school' of Indian writing. Unlike many writers of the South Asian diaspora, Mistry "doesn't engage in manic polemics or god-filled heights of fancy; instead his stories are careful, patient accounts of people trying to find answers in a world that seldom offers any. Reading his simple, moving tales of struggle and affliction, you are less in the company of Salman Rushdie or Arundhati Roy than in the company of Victor Hugo, perhaps or Thomas Hardy."[4]

Family Matters (Faber and Faber, March 2002) offers an excellent portrait of an Indian Parsi firmly, struggling to deal with their ageing father ailing with Parkinson's disease. Beautifully paced and superbly crafted, it chronicles an intricate account of domestic conflict. Set in Bombay in the 1990s, the novel "tells the story of familial love and affection, of personal and political corruption, the religious complexity, the power of memory to keep truth alive, and the ultimate peril of memory denied."[5] The story centres round a 79 year old Parsi widower, Nariman. A former professor of English, Nariman suffers from Parkinson's and a number of other debilitating diseases of age. He lives in a 7-room apartment in the complex called Chateau Felicity, with his two grown-up stepchildren: Coomy a bitter woman who seems intent on plaguing Nariman with rules 'to govern every aspect of his shrunken life' (2) and her brother Jal, a mild-mannered good-for-nothing fellow.

When the novel opens, Nariman feels a 'vague pang of abandonment' before he rises to prepare for his evening walk, much against the wishes of his stepchildren—Jal's reminding him of the hazards of walking, pot holes, lawlessness on the streets of Bombay and Nariman's answer, 'Ditches, potholes, traffic cannot extinguish all the joy of life.' (3) Nariman goes out and returns home with 'abrasions on his elbow and forearm, and a limp' (6) as he falls while crossing the lane. Reprimanded by Coomy for not acting responsibly, Nariman warns her: 'In my youth, my parents controlled me, and destroyed those years, thanks to them I married your mother and wrecked my middle years. Now you want to torment my old age. I wont allow it.' (7) And Coomy's retort 'such lies! . . . you ruined Mamma's life and mine and Jal's. I will not tolerate a word against her.' (7) This reflects the complex nature of their relationship, their love and hate bickerings and bondings.

Life, thus, is not particularly happy at Chateau Felicity as Nariman and his ineffectual stepson Jal are continually verbally lashed by Coomy. Matters turn for the worse when Nariman has a serious fall breaking his ankle. After a brief stay at hospital, he comes home and is confined to bed. Looking after him becomes a tedious job. The need for bed pans and the resultant stink greatly upsets Coomy and she breaks down weeping, saying it is too much for her. 'Looking after Pappa had been hard enough when he was not bedridden.' (74) Jal advises her to inform Roxina, their half-sister, but Coomy brushes the idea aside as she didn't want a rush of Chenoys here, spending evening after evening, telling her how to nurse Pappa. Besides, she had no energy to be their hostess, 'offering tea and cold drinks between bedpan and basin.' (75) Coomy has many grievances against her stepfather—his treatment of her mother and his supposed favouritism towards his own daughter Roxana. She decides that he is best handed over to her half-sister. She silences Jal when he tries to remind her of filial duties: 'I don't owe Pappa anything. He didn't change my diaper or wash my bum, and I don't have to clear his shit either.' (82) Both of them carry Nariman in an ambulance and dump him at the door of Roxana unannounced, confident that the loving daughter will welcome her father in, despite the fact that her family of four lives in a tiny two-room apartment in the complex called Pleasant Villa which Nariman had bought for her as a marriage gift.

Nariman's arrival at the tiny flat shared by Roxana, her husband Yezad and their two sons—Jehangir and Murad, opens the door to family conflict, tension and disruption. Yezad's job at a sports equipment store only pays enough to keep the family together and the addition of an elderly relative with attendant medical bills increases the pressure. Besides the scarcity of food and space, there are the realities of bodily decrepitude. Bowel movements and bedpans, stinks and sores become 'not only a helpless old man's cross to bear but a burden to those who love him most.'

Meanwhile, as the weakening Nariman tries not to be a burden to Roxana, he mumbles in his dreams, night after night, which gradually reveals the pain and secrets at the heart of the family. Mistry uses the device of flashback in italics at intervals to reveal the painful past of Nariman. As a young man, Nariman challenged the hierarchy of the Parsi faith he was born into by falling in love with a Goan Christian, Lucy. But due to his own weak will and lack of courage, he bowed to the relentless pressure of the 'marriage arrangers, the wilful manufactures of misery' (85) and married Yasmin, a widowed Parsi woman who had two children—Jal and Coomy. It was a joyless marriage, the only joy in their marriage being Roxana, the daughter they conceived together. Lucy, however, never stopped loving Nariman often coming by his house, staring up at his window longingly and eventually demeaning herself by taking up ayah's job at the house of Nariman's hostile neighbour, Arjani. Nariman felt compelled to go and meet her. This upset Yasmin greatly and led to a significant amount of animosity between husband and wife and kids. The end of this scandalous relationship was very tragic—both Yasmin and Lucy fall from the terrace to death. The whole drama of the novel stems from this. Nariman-Lucy relationship, even as "Mistry's touch here is very delicate and reserved and the melodramatic core of the story is revealed almost as an aside, in the epilogue."[5]

Nariman's proposed three-week stay at Pleasant Villa prolongs as Coomy pushes Jal into wrecking part of their apartment so that they will have the perfect excuse of not taking their stepfather back. The drama of pseudo-repair, which involves the help of their awesomely incompetent handiman neighbour, leads to a terrible accident resulting in Coomy's death. Roxana's family, meanwhile, reverts to subterfuges to survive financially. Yezad hatches doomed plans to raise money to fill the almost empty envelopes Roxana keeps in a drawer from which to pay the family expenses. Guilt and failure become Yezad's constant companions and prompt his fanatical return to religion.

Jal approaches Yezad with a plan. 'The solution,' said Jal, 'was for the whole family, along with Pappa to move into Chateau Felicity. It would be best for all of them. Also a way to honour Coomy's memory—something good at last after years of unhappiness (428). They dispose of their apartment at Pleasant Villa for forty lakhs, use a part of the amount to repair Chateau Felicity where they finally move along with the bedridden Nariman. A hospital ayah is hired to nurse him. Instead she gives him horrible bedsores, and is sent packing by Roxana. A wardboy in his thirties is hired as a replacement. A year after moving into Chateau felicity, Nariman dies with a 'serene expression' on his face.

There are quite a few sub-plots revealing the encroachments of a vicious, corrupting world. The troubles in Roxana's house are paralleled in the city of Bombay, ruled by the gangsters like Shiv Sena, who oppress Muslims as they preserve India from western festivities and morals. A substantial portion of the story unfolds at the Bombay Sporting Goods Emporium, where Yezad's boss Mr. Kapur decides to run in the next Municipal election to save his beloved, adopted city; who insists all faiths be celebrated in his shop and is eventually killed by the Shiv Sena for his abusive behaviour. There is also an echo of sectarian intolerance in orthodox Parsis' obsession with purity, fearing extinction through inter-marriage or migration. The novel both affirms Zoroastrian ritual and derides bigotry. Though the sceptic Yezad returns to the fold, his insistence that his sons marry

Parsis threatens in to replicate Nariman's tragedy. Yet while his family is baffled by this 'non-stop' praying stranger," (487) the reader is aware that Yezad's fundamentalism is born of guilt—yet another response to a corrupting world."[6]

But the focus throughout is on the struggles of the family; their binding ties and the trials they have to suffer through. Mistry's humanism reveals itself in the depiction of a family who are closer and loving in spite of all their differences. There are shades of King Lear in the novel. Nariman himself says, 'To so many classes I taught Lear, learning nothing myself. What kind of teacher is that, as foolish at the end of his life as at the beginning?' (190) Banished by Coomy who is the custodian of all her stepfather's retirement money, the elderly patriarch, like King Lear, is forced to seek the generosity of his progeny Roxana, who welcomes him in spite of her tight space and resources. The ailing patriarch has only this to say, 'Can care and concern he made compulsory? Either it resides in the heart or nowhere.' (116)

Caring the old, the novel stresses, is not only a measure of our humanity but a means of grasping it thoroughly. In the hospital, Nariman, pondering over an older orderly, wonders if collecting faeces and urine from the beds of the lane and the halt and the diseased might be the necessary conditions for achieving enlightenment.' (57) When Yezad loses his cool over the need and cares of Nariman, Roxana reminds him of Gandhi's teachings, 'that there was nothing nobler than the services of the weak, the old, the unfortunate,' (278) Mistry reveals, in a moving way, small triumphs of humanity over distaste, minute shifts that beacon leaps of compassion. Roxana beams with joy that 'our children can learn about old age, about caring—it will prepare them for life, make them better human beings.' (278) Yezad also comes to realize that, with death, helping one's elders through it is the only way to learn to take on one's own. As Roxana watches her nine year old son feeding 79 years old grandfather, the boy wiping a stray grain of rice from his lips. 'She felt she was witnessing something almost sacred.' (108) There's a subdued note of optimism at the end of the novel.

'Aren't you happy?' Roxana asks her youngest son. 'Yes,' he answers, 'I'm happy.' (487) "Family matters can be difficult, and Mistry doesn't shy away from showing, in all their roughness, the real truths about them."[7] There are trying situations, there are trials and ordeals but the ties of the family ultimately survive.

The novel does have some overtones of a morality tale. 'Trifling peccadilloes like a class monitor taking money or Yezad getting two stage actors to pose as people from the Shiv Sena and frighten his boss bring about a terrible nemesis.' Asked about the role of destiny in the novel, Mistry answered: "There is enough in the book to support the notion of destiny and enough to show that every thing happens as a result of what the characters choose to do. If Yezad had not undertaken the scheme with the actors, everything would have been different, Mr. Kapur would not have been killed. If Coomy had listened to her brother and said, right, 30 years have gone by, it is time to forgive and forget, things could have gone differently. It is the choice of each character that leads to the denouement."[8]

A master of telling detail, Rohinton Mistry has created a 'beautifully realized world.' with all too human characters. Hardly any character is uni-dimensional, except perhaps the very funny Villie cardmaster, the Matka woman. There are some unforgettably decent characters, like the beautiful Daisy, the violinist, who leaves her concert rehearsal, and dressed in glittering black, rushes to play Schubert's 'serenade' for Nariman as he lies dying.

Written in a flawless style with a well-knit plot, *Family Matters* has "all the richness, the compassion, the gentle humour, and the narrative sweep that have earned Rohinton Mistry the highest of accolades and prizes around the world."[9] Drawing a fine balance between skepticism and a affirmation, faith and bigotry, family nurture and control, Mistry has "once again given us something absolutely painfully pleasurable, a bitter sweet rendition of life in its most ordinary intimate setting." [10]

NOTES

1. *The Independent*, April 14, 2002.
2. Michael Ondaatjee, Guardian Unlimited@GuardianNewspapers limited, accessed on October 7, 2002.
3. Jane Seyed, *Coast Reporter,* May 19, 2002
4. Michael Ondaatjee, *Guardian Unlimited.*
5. Keki N. Daruwalla, *The Hindustan Times*, New Delhi, Sunday May 26, 2002.
6. Maya Jaggi, *The Guardian,* Saturday April 13, 2002 (Accessed on Oct 7, 2002).
7. Charles Foray *The Times*, 10 June 2002.
8. An Interview with Rohinton Mistry, *Canadian Fiction Magazine,* (http.com.aceessed on 7 Oct 2002.
9. Julia Flynn, *Sunday Star Times*, May 5, 2002, Accessed on Oct. 7, 2002.
10. Margie Thomson, *NZ Herald*, May 25, 2002.

Towards the Centre: The Writings of Uma Parameswaran

S. INDIRA
Dr. L.B. College, Visakhapatnam

Diasporic writing requires the writer's projection of his own culture, relating at the same time more positively to the host culture. As he moves from one culture to another, the writer may need to relocate himself afresh in relation to the centre. Living on margins, trying to perform the role of an ambassador and a refugee, the diasporic writer seeks affirmation and reaffirmation in a new perspective. Being an immigrant of 1960s, Uma Parameswaran, an Indo-Canadian writer, fulfils both the requirements of Diaspora. While the 'melting pot' ethos of the American culture helps to iron out the socio-cultural differences to a great extent, creating a monolithic 'American' identity, the multicultural 'mosaic' of Canadian culture protects the rights of ethnic cultures to maintain distinctive identities within the mainstream Canadian culture. Hence, she could relate more positively to Canadian culture, while retaining at the same time, her distinctive Indian identity.

Commenting on the creative process of immigrant literature, Uma Parameswaran has observed: "Every immigrant transplants part of his native land in the new country and the transplant may be said to have taken root once the immigrant figuratively sees the river that runs in the adopted place, not the Ganga or the Assiniboine as the Ganga, both of which imply a transference or substitution—the confluence of any two rivers is sacred."[1] Evidently the suggestion is that the Ganga and the Assiniboine cannot be substituted for one another but can exist as correlatives. The visualization of his experience and the concretization of the immediate in radically different idiom is indeed a process towards the relocation of the immigrant's identity. The New World presented is not a fantasy that cancels the reality of the past but on the contrary, it is a readjustment, adaptation, participation and fulfillment.

A study of Uma Parameswaran's work reflects the ongoing involvement of an immigrant writer with reality. Her first short story "The Door I Shut Behind Me"[2] (1967) reflects the sense of wonder and fear of the immigrant at the new world around himself, and nostalgia for the world left behind. The story is about a young graduate Chander who secures a green card and goes to Canada and his first impressions of being in a new country. While his mother gives him a copy of the *Ramayana* and a translation of *Bhagvad Gita* as parting gifts, he buys a copy of Chandra Sekhar's Radioactive Transfer, though it was not his field of study, nor was it one that one could read during a journey. He simply was driven by an urge to hold that book: "To see what it was to think of its India-born author, and to think of him was to open a world of ambition and inspiration." (105) He was quite surprised to see that the Indian families in Canada not only create "Little Indias" around themselves but also prefer to live in the memories of India of their childhood rather than the India of today. He comes to know that "when we leave our country we shut many doors behind ourselves though we are not aware of it at the time." (105) At the same time, being optimistic, he feels that "there are many doors ahead of us." (105)

Uma Parameswaran's second and most important work *Trishanku* (1988)[3] was a sequence of poems covering twenty years and spoken by various voices, where one finds an encounter of different cultures. In a review of the sequence, Tom Wayman pays tribute to its "startling and powerful collage of the experience of uprooting and resettlement, of the intermingling of personal and social histories and of many other human dimensions involved in transplanting an ancient culture to a new land." Within this context, the range of topics which Uma Parameswaran treats is far-reaching: child-birth and child-rearing, education, marriage and the family, death, friendship, community and poetry itself. The most striking feature of *Trishanku* is the vivid sense of life created by the memories, dreams and present reality of each speaker.

Here are a few voices that depict the fear, wonder, the uncertainty, the dilemmas, the sense of loss, anger, isolation, despair, intense nostalgia, and at the same time an overriding impulse to survive in the new environment. The collective memory touches every person who is physically, culturally and emotionally displaced. The characters recur in all her work—Chander, Usha, Chandrika, Dilip, Savitri, Sharad, Jayant—caught in between the worlds like "Trishanku," trying to create a third space.

Chandrika: Madras, I love you
Your broad beach road where the polished tar
Flings mirages that vapor on my speeding car
Your sands stretched out beside the sea
Where at my feet laps eternity
Madras, I hope one day to call me your own
Though pledged now to the land
Which my love has made our home (29)

Chander: Go break, my heart
What do I care?
Hardly remember you as mine
Gave you so long ago to her
And kept the empty shrine
Polished and perfumed
An eunuch dusting the corridors of time
Hoping
Fondly hoping
She'd give me hers to place there in
Go break, my heart
I have no tears to spare
For a stranger (19)

Uma Parameswaran provides a new perspective based on gender to the whole discourse of diasporic writing. Here is Chandrika willing to bond with the land to which her husband Chander has brought her and can love both homelands. But Chander cannot commit himself to either. "Perhaps women with centuries of cultural indoctrination and expectation are able to adapt more quickly and to accept and love two homes without conflict or ambivalence."[4]

Sharad: In our ancestral home
Every new moon day
Father, as his father before him in silk dhoti
Vibhuti on forehead and chest
Sacred thread dipped in turmeric
Sat on a wooden plank
facing the east
to repeat the Purohit's chant
Sprinkle holy water with darbha grass
and call upon our ancestors
But here the sun rises south east
And the planets are all—a Kilter
and all my words questions. (33)

Dilip the Child: Amma, I like school
It is such fun
We play most of the time
and sing songs in French
Ma, you think you could change my name
To Jim or David or something?
When the snow comes, Ma,
I'll get less brown, won't I?
It would be nice to be white
more like everyone else, you know?
I can do everything on the Jungle-gym
That Petey can (32)

Savitri: It scares me, this other world
that intrudes on me
of a sudden
in everyday actions (69)

Usha: Long ago
into my dark chamber
the sun shone thro a crack
danced madly
withdrew
left me
more alone
than ever
I had been (23)

Chandrika: Across the seas is a land
where man may stand tall
May walk and talk without fear
May pray and play in freedom
I have been there, my brother,
The land is green but my heart was barren
Warm are the people but my heart was lonely
Money flows in rivers but my heart was dry
Bereft of want and tensions
Bereft of sorrow and pain
Bereft of comradeship
My heart lost its voice, my brother
It is not the land for you and me.

Chandrika: I heard him come in the door
and straight to the kitchen
He had snowflakes in his hair
And his face was white as any neighbour
all blood formed an instant puddle
as he stood at the kitchen door
Gangajal, he said, I need Gangajal

The cry for the Gangajal has particular meaning for Indo-Canadian readers, but the poem's capacity to move readers of all cultural backgrounds typifies the broad appeal of *Trishanku*. Vithal who represents the promising younger generation, says assertively,

> We shall build our temple
> Here where the Assiniboine
> Flows into the Red
> And I shall bring Ganga
> As Bhagiratha did of old,
> to our land,
> our Assiniboine
> And the flute player
> Dark as Kaya blossom
> Shall dance on the waters of La Salle (79)

The flute player. Lord Krishna does come to the alien soil when Uma Parameswaran stages "Meera" written in 1971. It has a simple story line that takes us through Meera's life with all its familiar episodes. It gives us the pleasure of the familiar, while telling the outsiders basic details about Krishna's life and our dance and music traditions. "Sita's Promise" another dance-drama, written by Uma Parameswaran, links epic India with modern Canada through myth and dance. Rama, Sita and Lakshmana—the main characters in the *Ramayana*—during their forest exile find a wounded Arctic term that has lost its way in its northern migration. They resolve to take it back to its home, they travel northwards, through India to the Himalayas, where Jatayu, the sacred eagle, carries them to the tern's home by the shores of the primeval ocean that we now call Lake Agassiz. The native children dance for Sita and ask her to stay with them. Sita says she must go but promises them that she will come again, "I, through my people, shall surely come again, and we shall sing songs with the children of all the different lands who make this their home." (23-24)

"Sita's Promise" and "Meera" indicate the nostalgic passion of an expatriate writer to represent the characters and message from the greatest resources of her native culture with the help of her talent and learning and to represent them to an alien audience, earning from them, if possible, the same love and regard that she carried within her for the precious givens that lay beyond the door she shut behind her.

"Dear Deedi, My Sister," composed in the 1980s, reflects the writer's embracing a larger immigrant community as the *poems* are addressed by people not from India alone but from Nicaragua, Kenya, Philippines, Nigeria, Pakistan, Hong Kong, Sri Lanka and Japan. Like the poems in *Trishanku*, these poems too address the issues of racism, adjustment, adaptation and the hopes and despairs of the immigrants.

> We are new Canadians
> Come from faraway places
> The Alps and the Andes,
> Essequibo and the Gangas,
> Our memories, our faces
> Chiselled by ancient cultures
> Whose courses had been half run

Long ere cartier's had begun
We are new Canadians
Come from many races
Black, white, olive, brown
All alike, for all the many places
Hightech, midtech, notech
Are one
under a sky bluer than any we've seen
On snow whiter than ever we dreamed,
We stand beside the Golden Boy
Holding Golden sheafs of corn
Against a dawn heralding the joy
of years to come (72-73)

In spite of the pain of discrimination and alienation, Uma Parameswaran ends these poems with an affirmative vision. So, one agrees with Judith Kearns who says in her preface to *Shaktis Worlds*: "She [South Asian Canadian poet] is us, but a little newer and fresher and her poems are a little more honest and passionate than ours. If she has found a country, our country has found a poet."

This acceptance of and by the host culture amidst the dilemmas and self-imposed ghettoisation is clearly seen in Uma Parameswaran's play "Rootless but green are the Boulevard Trees." The dilemmas exist more in the parent generation than in the younger one. Here is Sharad saying, "It upsets me profoundly to find myself in a crowd. All these alien faces staring at or through you. It makes me wonder. What am I doing here? Who are these faceless people among whom my life is oozing away. Each so self-contained, so complete, looking at me as though I shouldn't be here. It's a strange, eerie feeling, all those discreetly questioning eyes that make me ask endless questions." (82) And Savitri says that's why she got herself a car so that she wouldn't have to ask herself all those questions, that perhaps can never be answered, not to their satisfaction. But the youngsters assert themselves and demand their inheritance. Jayant, one of the young men, knows that home is where the feet are. "Jayant: our people, our old country, Dad, there's no 'our people' and no 'old country' for anyone in the world anymore, least of all for us. This is our land and here we shall stay." (83) When the father distressingly points out the absence of roots, the son assures him that they can grow roots in their adopted land.

Jayant: Sure, Dad. Just look outside. The monstrous new apartment block out there—they have twenty-foot trees around the patio and there are five footers inside the quadrangle, all set up overnight and flourishing like crazy. (83)

Vithal: If the temp goes up to zero degree midweek, as they expect that would be the end of that (He waves at the tree). (127)

Jayant: So what? (vehemently) What does it matter how long it stands? The point is that it is there, beautiful and green for the length of its life? A day, a hundred thousand days, it is a question of what we do and are, during that time. (127)

In an article, Uma Parameswaran states: "Romanticizing one's native land has a place so long as it does not paralyze one's capacity to develop new bonds within one's adopted homeland.[9] The new bonds are already being forged between Jyoti and Andre and Vithal and Donna in "Rootless." Sharad and Savitri feel that "Andre is a decent boy. He behaves just like one of us. So respectful and he looks like us too, with his black hair and eyes." (81) "Donna is more Hindu than many of us." (104)

Jyoti, Jayant, Vithal, Swapna and such youngsters are the 'flags' planted by Uma Parameswaran in the Canadian soil who are going to create a new culture, a third space which transforms and enriches Canadian culture, while they themselves have travelled a long way from "unthinking scorn, unfeeling barbs, closed fists and closed hearts" to being accepted, appreciated and acculturated.

NOTES

1. Uma Parameswaran, "Ganga in the Assiniboine; Prospects for Indo-Canadian Literature," *A Meeting of the Streams* (Toronto: TSAR, 1985).
2. Uma Parameswaran, "Trishanku," "The Door I Shut Behind Me," *Trishanku and Other Writings* (New Delhi: Prestige 1998).

3. Uma Parameswaran, "Home is where your feet are and may your heart be those too!" *Writers of the Indian Diaspora*, ed. Jasbir Jain (Jaipur: Rawat, 1988), p. 32.
4. Uma Parameswaran, "Meera: A Dance Drama," "Sita's Promise: A Dance Drama"; "Dear Deedi, My Sister: Performance Piece for Voices," "Rootless but Green are the Boulevard Trees," *Sons Must Die and Other Plays.*

South Asian Canadian Point of View about Human Rights: Uma Parameswaran's "Dear Deedi, My Sister" and "Rootless but Green are the Boulevard Trees"

S. GANESAN
H.H. The Rajah's College, Pudukottai

Canada is famous for its multiculturalism. Critics often refer to the Canadian Mosaic. On the other hand, Canada has had a not so impressive track record in the area of Human Rights in the past. According to Michelle Falardeau Ramasày, "The early human rights laws were not particularly effective in combating discrimination, because they were based on a criminal model and were difficult to enforce. There were no special institutions developed to handle discrimination complaints . . . in a society where discrimination was both institutionalized and socially acceptable it was difficult to obtain a charge, let alone a conviction."[1]

For instance, the Jews were targeted and discriminated against. Even entry was denied to them in places like pubs and beaches. Also, one cannot forget the 'Komagata Maru incident.' In 1914, 376 immigrants boarded the ship Komagata Maru and reached the shores of Vancouver. But they were not allowed to disembark for days and finally barring a few, the majority was sent back by the then racist regime of Canada.

The first modern human rights law was adopted in Ontario in 1962. Through the 1960s and 1970s, provincial governments adopted human rights laws and established human rights commissions. In 1977, the parliament adopted the Canadian Human Rights Act. Also there were Acts prohibiting discrimination on grounds of nationality, ethnic origin and language. In spite of all these, even today the immigrants' condition is not so comfortable in Canada. They find it difficult to get suitable jobs. The case is more severe with the non-skilled workers. Also, at times, there are controversies arising out of their trying to maintain their religious identity. The recent controversy regarding the Sikh RCMP officers' right to wear turbans as part of their uniforms, is an example.

From time to time, the immigrant voices have registered their protest and their feelings against discrimination and the denial of their rights. This paper attempts a critical examination of Uma Parameswaran's plays "Dear Deedi, My Sister" and "Rootless but Green are the Boulevard Trees." Apart from other issues, these speak out on the discrimination practised against immigrants. The play "Dear Deedi, My Sister" is in the mode of correspondence between two sisters, one living in Canada and the other in India. Apart from these two, we come across a variety of men and women, all immigrants from various parts of the world, settled in Canada. Life in the new land places them in an uncomfortable condition. They are overawed by the vastness of the new landscape and baffled by the new aggressive cultural surroundings. Sekoni, a young immigrant, seated in a bus, wonders:

> Who are these faceless people
> Among whom my life is oozing away?
> Each is so self-assured,
> Glancing swiftly but completely,
> Through me, wordlessly asking:
> Why are you here?
> And the bus moves on and we. (65)

Even a little schoolboy from the Philippines, Ilago, like Blake's Little Black Boy, has been conditioned by the racism prevalent in the society. He says:

> When the snow comes, Ma,
> I'll get less brown, wont I?
> It would be nice to be white,
> More like everyone else. (65)

More importantly, jobs are denied to the immigrants. Even in educational institutions, their children are discriminated against. All this makes the immigrants feel disillusioned. They cry out in anguish:

> It will not be easy, some said,
> And it has not, as we all know,
> Who have worked hard, or worse still,
> Have no work at all, though willing
> And waiting for the break
> That would set us on our own
>
> What we were not told, never guessed,
> Is written on our children's faces
> Furrowed with tears because of our race
> Or colour, or tongue that stumbles
> Over words so alien to the many places
> From which we've come.
>
> Have we come from the Niger and Luzon
> From the Antilles and Hong Kong,
>
> Only to see our young ones' faces
> Slapped by unthinking scorn, unfeeling barbs,
> From closed fists and closed hearts. (72-73)

The play ends with an old couple, originally from Somalia, still feeling optimistic of future in Canada which is based more on their inherent confidence than on concrete facts.

In "Rootless but Green are the Boulevard Trees" , the Bhaves, a Maharashtrian family migrates to Canada, leaving a well-settled pattern of life back home. Sharad, who was comfortably placed at home as an Atomic Energy Scientist, migrates to Canada, "to live without tension and yet with dignity, to give our children good food, a liberal education, a healthy environment where, because the body doesn't have to scrounge for sustenance, the spirit can aspire to higher experiences than this sorry world allows." (77) But in Canada, he couldn't get a suitable job and ends up as a real-estate broker and encyclopaedia seller, much to the derision of his own son.

For all his optimism behind his migration, Sharad has to come across many unpleasant situations. While narrating his experience in a bus, he says:

> It upsets me profoundly to find myself in a crowd. All these alien faces staring at or through you. It makes me wonder. Makes me ask myself, what am I doing here? Who are these faceless people among whom my life is oozing away? Each so self-contained, so complete, looking at me as though I shouldn't be there. (82)

Veejala, Sharad's sister, is an Assistant Professor in a Canadian University. The insipid academic scenario in her institution and the colour-cum-gender bias practised against her, makes her quit her plum post. The newspaper report goes like this:

> Dr. Veejala Moghe, assistant professor of astronomy, has resigned her faculty position . . . claims this is a back wood . . . where nothing of significance has been done or can be done in her faculty. . . . Asked if she felt she had been discriminated against because of her sex, Dr. Moghe said, "I happen to be of the wrong colour as well." (110)

The younger generation of immigrants keenly feel their predicament. They have no hope of assimilating with the Canadian mainstream, for, the whites don't want to mingle with them. Some of the youngsters even prefer to follow the example set by the Jews long back, that is, living in ghettoes, as a close-knit community to achieve progress. One youngster points out the fact that once one achieves success and gets accepted by the mainstream, one may lose one's roots in the process. In other words, during the process of assimilation, the immigrant feels the danger of a sort of pseudo-complacency creeping in and creativity getting stilled and the ethnic identity getting erased.

In recent years, there has been a debate on whether to allow multiculturalism or to urge the various ethnic groups to assimilate with the Canadian mainstream. If various ethnic groups are given equal rights and opportunities, as enjoyed by the whites, definitely they can realize their potential. Possibly, while retaining their own ethnic identity, the ethnic groups can come together and feel the 'one Canadian identity' on important issues, thus effectively contributing to the 'Canadian cause.'

NOTES

1. Ramasay Falardeau Michelle, "Promoting Equality in a Multicultural Society: The Canadian Experience," *Indian Journal of Canadian Studies*, volume VII, 1998, p. 3.
2. Uma Parameswaran, *Sons Must Die and Other Plays* (New Delhi: Prestige, 1998).

In Search of 'Roots': A Study of Uma Parameswaran's "Rootless but Green are the Boulevard Trees"

JYOTI JAKHAR DAHIYA
P.G.D.A.V. (E) College
University of Delhi

> Wandering between two worlds, one dead,
> the other powerless to be born
>
> Matthew Arnold, *Stanzas from the Grande Chartreuse*

> Your country [India] has moved from brain drain to brain gain. Indians own over 750 companies in Silicon Valley alone.
>
> President Clinton, Hi-Tec City, Hyderabad, March 2000

The above statements reflect the truth and complexity of the Indian Diaspora. Like the members of any other Diaspora, Indians in a Diasporic situation face the problems of alienation and partial assimilation in the new land. Yet, many of them have achieved powerful positions and have made an important presence in the new land for instance, S.R. Nathan, the President of Singapore, is an Indian by origin. Indians have made their presence felt in every field. In the US, 39 percent of doctors, 36 percent of NASA employees, 34 percent of Microsoft staff are Indians. (*The Sunday Times of India*, August 13, 2000) However the other side of the coin is that life has not been easy for the Diasporic people in the alien environment. The last year attacks on the people of the Indian and Bangladeshi origin in the UK delineate the fact. The present paper therefore attempts to comprehend this complexity through an analysis of Uma Parameswaran's "Rootless but Green are the Boulevard Trees."

Uma Parameswaran, born in 1941 in Madras in India, is a successful writer and has been teaching in the University of

Winnipeg, Canada since 1967. She has to her credit books of literary criticism like *Cyclic Hope Cyclic Pain*, *SACLIT: An Introduction to South-Asian-Canadian Literature*, collections of short stories like *Maru and the Maple Leaf*, collections of poetry like *Trishanku* and plays like *Sons Must Die and Other Plays*, "Rootless but Green are the Boulevard Trees." She is a member of the vibrant Indo-Canadian Diaspora and voices her experiences and feelings in her literary works.

The present paper is a study of Parameswaran's play, "Rootless but Green are the Boulevard Trees." The attempt is to look at those aspects of the play that assist in formulating her views on the Indo-Canadian Diaspora. The following discussion would examine Uma Parameswaran's viewpoint on various issues—the question of identity of a Diasporic person; nature of the 'new homeland'; differences between the first-generation migrants and the second-generation migrants; issues of assimilation, racism, non-acceptance, rootlessness; the notion of 'multiculturalism'—as evident from the play. A comparison of her views with those of critics and theorists like Vijay Mishra, Salman Rushdie, Bhiku Parekh, Jasbir Jain is presented to bring forth a profound understanding of the predicament of the Diasporic people.

The play is set in Winnipeg, during March-April 1979. In the play the lives of the members of the two families of Indian origin—the Bhave family and the Moghe family—are evinced. They are the members of the 'New' Diaspora to use Vijay Mishra's term. Critics like Uma Parameswaran and Vijay Mishra have acknowledged that in order to develop a better understanding of Indian Diaspora, it is expedient to divide it into two groups or "two very distinct waves of emigration" (*SACLIT*, 5) as these two groups have migrated under different conditions and because of discrete reasons. Vijay Mishra examines the Indian Diaspora through its two phases which he calls "pre-modern phase"/Old Diaspora and "late modern phase"/New Diaspora. The first phase includes the movement of indentured labourers, which took place in the nineteenth century. The second phase includes migration of the people of Indian origin to different parts of the world especially to metropolitan centres of North America, Europe and Australia in more recent times. The characters of this play are members of the New Diaspora who have migrated to Canada voluntarily to be successful materially. The members of the Bhave family are: Sharad, the father, Savitri, the mother, and their three children—Jayant, Krish and Jyoti. The Moghe family has: Veejala, Sharad's sister, Anant, Veejala's husband, and their children Vithal and Priti (or Prixie). Other characters of the play are Arun, Dilip, Rajen, and Sridhar, all Indo-Canadians and friends of Jayant and Vithal; Andre, Jyoti's boyfriend and Laura, Priti's friend are non-hyphenated Canadians.

The play is set in the Bhave home. The play presents a couple of days from the lives of these characters. Their life style, their problems, their predicaments, their experiences, their past, their hopes, find a mention in the play. In the subsequent sections of this paper, I propose to study those aspects of the play which are relevant for an understanding of the Indo-Canadian Diaspora.

II

The first section of the second part of the paper discusses the multifarious aspects of the lives of the first generation migrants (from India)—Savitri, Sharad, Veejala and Anant. The attempt is to study Parameswaran's portrayal of these members of the Indo-Canadian Diasporic community and to understand how they reflect the ethos of the same. *Encyclopedia of Cultural Anthropology* defines Diasporic communities as "those communities, migrant populations, ethnicities, or nations that, although separated from their home terrains (either forcibly or voluntarily) and scattered among other communities, imaginatively preserve and regenerate a set of distinctive cultural or ethnic identities. Members of diasporic communities often feel that they are not fully accepted by their host societies and regard their place of origin as their ideal home, to which they will someday return when conditions improve. As a result, they directly or vicariously maintain solidarity with their homeland and create a collective memory, or myth, about their historical achievements in that place." (341)

Another concept which can direct us to a better comprehension of the characters of this play is that of 'Hybrid.' The term 'Hybrid' is well defined in *A Dictionary of Cultural and Critical Theory*: "The term 'hybrid' is commonly assumed to be anything of mixed origin, of unlike parts . . . in literary and cultural studies it refers to the idea of occupying in-between space; that is, of being of many, composite, or syncretic entities, new formations, Creole or intermixed peoples." (251) These theoretical insights can facilitate our understanding of the complex issues and experiences associated with the lives of the first generation migrants in this play.

In the play Jayant, Sharad's son, introduces his father. His father was an atomic energy scientist in India. Jayant believes that instead of migrating to Canada if he would have stayed in India, he would have been a Director by now. Jayant's voice has contempt for his father as he chose to migrate. He says bitterly: "Instead he quits the place to be and rots here selling houses, Jeesus, a crappy real estate broker, just one step better than an encyclopedia salesman." (76) Though he had a better career in India, the living conditions are better in Canada which even Jayant admits later when he recalls their ancestral house back home: "Some house that, a sprawling shambles handed down untouched from the time of Peshwa, where you have to walk half a mile to get to the shithouse, Jeesus, we haven't lost anything on that count; even he couldn't think so." (77)

Jayant suggests that though materially they are much better here, Sharad does not enjoy a good status in this foreign land. Sustaining in a new land has not been very easy for him. Jyoti enumerates the hardships Sharad had faced: "It couldn't have been easy for him to move out after he was thirty-five, and it is no bed of roses here, mowing the lawn and painting the house and a hundred menial chores which were done by servants in the luxury of family back home." (77) Therefore, the play proposes that Sharad had to sacrifice a respectable job for securing a comfortable life.

Like the others in the play, Sharad too experiences racial anxiety. He has a lean face and a long neck "which he tends to stick out so that his Adam's apple shows even clearer and he looks even taller than he is." (80-81) Sharad's life represents the state of Diasporic dilemma as along with better living conditions and material success, Canada also offers racism. Sharad is like "Trishanku." "Trishanku" is a figure from Indian mythology—and a symbol used by Uma Parameswaran—who, with the efforts of the 'rishis' was pushed to the heaven but was denied entrance to the heaven by the gods. With both the forces working simultaneously in opposite directions, he could not belong to either place and stayed in between two worlds. His plight of not being able to belong anywhere gets further reflected in his behaviour vis-à-vis his children. As a father he finds it difficult to accept his children's life style. In a conversation with his wife, Savitri, he justifies Jyoti's actions more to himself than to his wife:

> Don't be a worrier, Savi. She is a good girl, and Andre is a decent boy. He behaves just like one of us. So respectful. And looks like us too, with his black hair and eyes . . . the youngsters here are doing well. They have their own code of morals and they are more idealistic than we give them credit for. The disco craze is perfectly harmless. . . . A hundred youngsters swaying around; group activities are safety valves that this generation has discovered for itself. As long as they are in a group, they are alright. And thank God for our Winnipeg winters; nobody can wander into the bushes. Least of all our children. (81)

Sharad's speech reflects his apprehensions and anxieties. He cannot reconcile with the idea that his daughter has a non-Indian boyfriend and stresses that he behaves and looks like 'one of us' ("black hair and eyes"). He knows a little about the "disco craze" and refuses to acknowledge that his children can do anything 'immoral' ("nobody can wander into the bushes. Least of all our children"). Sharad is aware of the activities the young Canadians engage in but he is not willing to accept that his children can be a part of those. He wants his children to be the members of the Canadian society and at the same time wants them to confirm to his notion of Indian children.

Savitri, Sharad's wife is another first generation immigrant who leads a dual life. She is a Canadian only on the surface. This is emphasized in her manner of dressing also. When outside, she dresses up like any other Canadian—in boots, coat, pant-suit and when she is back home, "she has kumkum on her forehead . . . [and] comes in, tucking the pleats of her sari at her waist. She looks different now, very brown, very Indian." (79-80)

Like Sharad, she also faces challenges in the new country but of a different nature. One of them is to deal with her daughter, Jyoti. Jyoti has been brought up in Canada and has adopted the 'Canadian' mannerisms. However, Savitri finds it difficult to accept that her unmarried daughter has an active sexual life. She reacts vehemently when she discovers an open condom pack in Sharad's car which was taken by Jyoti the night before. She says angrily, "we are supposed to treat you as rational adults even when you behave like beasts. I don't know whether you meant to flaunt this to your father or what, but I don't want this to happen in dad's car, ever. . . . I'll take you to Doctor MacRae and put you on the pill . . . if you haven't already of course." (90-91) The above reaction reflects her partial assimilation in the given condition. She is enraged and upset to know that her daughter is sleeping with her boyfriend but instead of pursuing her for discontinuation, she wants her to be safe ("on the pill") and does not want "this to happen in dad's car."

The idiosyncratic problems of the second-generation migrants forms the next section. There are a number of second-generation migrants in the play: Jyoti, Jayant, Krish, Vithal, Priti, Arun, Dilip, Rajen, and Sridhar. In the course of their discussions they raise many important issues like racism and multiculturalism in Canada; the questions of assimilation and alienation; rootlessness, their real home, and so on.

Jyoti brings forth one of the most common problems of the second-generation immigrants in Canada. Most of them have studied in the Canadian schools, speak like the other Canadians, dress up like other Canadians, have similar hobbies, but they are still seen as aliens. In a conversation with Jayant, she says:

> I sure hope it gets into that thick head of yours that we are different, and no matter what we do, we are never going to fit in here. Take to the road, get high, sleep around but still and all . . . all the expletives, all the in jargon, but you are never going to be one of the boys. Not that I see why anyone would want to fit into this mould. (76)

The second-generation Indo-Canadians find it difficult to maintain a balance between what the society expects from them and what is expected from them by their families. This gets manifested in Jyoti's character. She, probably like any other young Canadian girl, has a boyfriend and is sexually involved with him. However, she is aware of the fact that this is completely unacceptable to her family members. Her father refuses to admit that his children "can wander into the bushes." (81) Savitri is infuriated when she discovers an "open condom pack" (90) from the car Jyoti used the night before. Jyoti's brother, Jayant is also upset when he realizes that his sister might be sleeping with her boyfriend. In a conversation with Jyoti, he makes a reference to getting laid. Soon after that "he looks at her, and there is something in her eye that draws him up sharply against the wall of recognition." (77) He is extremely disturbed and wants her to turn down his suspect. "Unwilling to accept it," he desperately wants her to deny the same: "You haven't sis? You haven't?" (78)

On one hand Jyoti's mother and brother are disturbed to discover her involvement and on the other hand, Andre, Jyoti's boyfriend, is also not very happy with her. Her rejection of his invitation to go out infuriates him and before leaving, he says: "One day I'll get into your inner kernel of stillness. I swear I will tear my way into that silence and hear you scream of lust and pain. . . . I know you are a cauldron of emotions sealed four times over." (118)

Jyoti exemplifies many others who are unable to handle pressure from home and friends. As a result, her irritability and unhappiness surfaces. Sharad notices the "seeds of sadness in her eyes" (81) and the reason of her melancholy is her unsuccessful attempt to fit in in the given environment.

Unlike their parents, the second-generation migrants do not feel in tandem with the 'homeland.' Uma Parameswaran's concept of 'Four Phases in the total Canadian immigrant experience' is expedient to comprehend the reason. In an essay, "Ganga in the Assiniboine: Prospects for Indo-Canadian Literature" published in *A Meeting of Streams: South Asian Canadian Literature*, Parameswaran elaborates on all the four phases: "The first is that in which the primary and overriding component is a consciousness of the vastness and harshness of the Canadian landscape." (83) The second phase is seen by the author as "the struggle of immigrants to establish themselves in their own esteem and in society. They brave the landscape and climate; they overcome their nostalgia, and usually, despite hardships and prejudice, they establish themselves in their new land." (83-84) The third phase is seen as one "in which second-generation Canadians, fed on monstrous meat, the fabled splendour of an idealized homeland, make a journey—inner or actual—and then realize that home is here, not elsewhere." (85) The fourth phase is "the affirmation that home is here but 'here' is not exclusively English or even English-French territory into which one has to fit in, but a place where one can be oneself, assimilating if one is comfortable doing so, being different if one chooses to be so." (85)

As the third phase suggests, unlike the first-generation migrants, the second-generation migrants feel that their home is here (Canada), not elsewhere (India). The difference in perspective of the first-generation and second-generation migrants gets reflected in a dialogue between Sharad and his son Jayant:

Jayant: Our people, our old country, Dad, there is no "our people" and no "old country" for anyone in the world any more, least of all for us. This is our land and we shall stay.

Sharad: Roots, son, roots. Can we really grow roots here?

Jayant: Sure, Dad, just look outside. The monstrous new apartment block out there—they have twenty-foot trees around the patio and there are five-footers inside the quadrangle, all set up overnight and flourishing like crazy. If anything, the pollution in the air seems to have acted like pep pills. (83)

As Jayant reflects in his speech, which the title of the play reinforces, the second-generation migrants cannot relate to the homeland' in the same way as the first-generation migrants do. The second-generation immigrants identify themselves with the Canadians and not with the Indians. Jayant argues:

> Why should we fall on the neck of bastards who'd be way out of our orbit in India? One makes one's friends for their qualities . . . not for their skin colour. Face it, man, we don't have anything in common with the other half of the Indians here. Why the hell do we have to rub shoulders with them simply because we happen to come from the same political entity? . . . Why in sacred hell, give me one solid reason in hell, why should we paw around with illiterates who troop into airports carrying kerosene tins and bedding rolls? (99-100)

A number of issues of direct relevance to the second-generation migrants are discussed in a conversation among Jayant's friends—Arun, Sridhar, Rajen, Vithal, and Dilip. Arun voices his observation that the Indian girls run after the whites. In the course of the discussion, Jyoti suggests that there is a need for all of them to change: "we have to change with time. Haven't we been in the closet long enough?" (97) One can see that the second-generation immigrants desperately want to belong to Canada. They rarely show any urge to go back to India. They are willing to change with time. Though they are 'rootless' in the new land, they want to flourish and want to be 'green.'

The next section attempts to probe into the issues of alienation, assimilation and 'nostalgic trips.' Most of the members of the Indo-Canadian Diaspora experience these feelings.

As the notable six characteristics of William Safran's definition of Diaspora also suggest, the memory of the homeland remains an important part of (especially the first generation) members of Indo-Canadian Diaspora. The attempt is to keep strong ties with the past. Salman Rushdie makes an interesting observation on the nature of past and memory in *Imaginary Homelands*. He discusses *Midnight's Children* as "a novel of memory and about memory, so that my India was just that: 'my' India . . . I tried to make it as imaginatively true as I could, but imaginative truth is simultaneously honourable and suspect, and I knew that my India may only have been one to which I . . .was willing to admit I belonged." (10) The narrator of *Midnight's Children*, Saleem has selective, incorrect, fragmented memory and his memory in some ways becomes a representative of that of the Diasporic people. While memory of the homeland becomes a 'tool' for the Diasporic writers, it stays an important part of the lives of the Diasporic people. The characters of "Rootless but Green are the Boulevard Trees" too go on 'nostalgic trips.' They remember their 'homeland,' old friends, relatives and house and this brings the realization of being isolated in the new land. A distant vision of the comforts of the 'homeland' coupled with the prevalent racism in the new land brings frustration. As a result, most of the members of the Indo-Canadian Diaspora experience the feelings of alienation and partial assimilation.

In the play, Sharad reveals to his son the reason for not using the public transport: "It upsets me profoundly to find myself in a crowd. All those alien faces staring at or through you. It makes me wonder. Makes me ask myself, What am I doing here? Who are these faceless people among whom my life is oozing away? Each so self-contained, so complete, looking at me as though I shouldn't be there. It's a strange, eerie feeling, all those discreetly questioning eyes that make me ask endless questions. . . [Savitri adds] that is why I got myself a car. So I wouldn't have to ask myself questions that perhaps never can be answered. Not to our satisfaction." (82)

As mentioned before, the sense of being partially assimilated is relatively more among the first-generation migrants. Jayant sees some hope as he mentions that 'rootless' trees can also grow and flourish. But Sharad is not comforted:

> That would be a most reassuring analogy, Jai, if our poplar hadn't died. . . . Looking at them, who'd think one of them was dead? . . . And if an Ontario poplar can't grow and survive in Manitoba soil, what chance do we have? (83)

The feeling of alienation aggravates with a vision of the 'homeland.' The diasporic people remember their 'homeland' in various ways. Recalling old myths; telling and retelling many versions of the stories from the great Indian epics to the children; cooking Indian food at home, are various ways by which the characters of this play maintain a relationship with their 'homeland.'

The level of the assimilation in the new land gets manifested also in the language the characters speak in the play. There is difference in the language of the first-generation and the second-generation migrants. The second-generation migrants like Krish, Jayant and Vithal speak in English filled with jargon like "howdee" (75), "Bug off, bozo" (75) and reference to "Jeesus." On the other hand, the first-generation migrants in the play, like Savitri and Veejala, use a lot of words from their mother tongue, like "beta." This difference in their language delineates that the first-generation migrants have assimilated partially and want to maintain connection with their native language and life. On the other hand, compared to the first-generation migrants, the second-generation migrants have assimilated in their new environment in a better way.

Assimilation in the new land is not easy because of feelings of nostalgia on the one hand and non-supportive circumstances in the new land on the other hand. The members of the Indo-Canadian Diaspora encounter racism everywhere and the Canadian government's policy of Multiculturalism is a sham.

There are many powerful literary pieces in Indo-Canadian writing which bring forth instances of racism. Some of them include Himani Bannerjee's poem "Paki Go Home" and Dilip's voice in Parameswaran's *Trishanku* which shows his racial anxiety when he says:

> Amma, I like schools
> It is such fun.
> We play most of the time
> And sing songs in French.
> . . . Ma, you think you could change my name
> to Jim or David or something?
> Amma I love recess time.
> . . . When the snow comes, Ma,

I'll get less brown won't I?
It would be nice to be white,
More like everyone else
you know? (32)

However the play under study just makes a few references to the issue. Vithal reveals to Arun that if the house of a non-white Canadian "gets stoned and eggs smashed on the window," one does not even get a fast response "from and goddam cop." (99)

But racism is not always that explicit. It is evident when "Whites would whitewash the white barbarism" (100) by re-writing the incidents like the 'Komagata Maru' incident. Vithal also points out: "do you read the story between the lines, the editorial slant of how quick they are to identify the colour and country of the few who get into trouble?" (101) One can notice by these extracts of the play that racism taints the lives of the Indo-Canadians.

III

This section offers to comprehend the reality of the policy of Multiculturalism in Canada. Multiculturalism means mosaic which esteems and values variances and pluralities. Multiculturalism has been the official, state policy of Canada since 1971. However most of the Diasporic writers believe that this is just a tag which was necessary politically and is not practised. In M.G.Vassanji's *No New Land*, a poet calls it 'multivulturalism.' (111)

Other Solitude: Canadian Multicultural Fictions, edited by Linda Hutcheon and Marion Richmond presents various viewpoints to the stated issue. The (political) rationale for the policy is that that with the advent of the people of diverse cultures to Canada, comes into interaction social tensions and cultural riches. And Multiculturalism tries to settle the space between the two. The motive quite admirable, "yet the fiction and the conversations [with the writers of the Diaspora] . . . show that even writers within the same racial or ethnic grouping often disagree on the function or success of multiculturalism as both policy and reality." (4)

In the play "Rootless but Green are the Boulevard Trees", Parameswaran presents multiple viewpoints vis-à-vis Multiculturalism through the voices of Dilip, Vithal, Rajen and Sridhar. Dilip believes that as one is in this new land, he/she should "try to assimilate" (98). Vithal, however, praises the Jews and believes that living in ghettos is a better idea than trying to assimilate:

> Assimilate, my ass. They don't want us to assimilate. They want us out. We'll be squashed like bugs soon. All these years we thought the isolation was coming from us, but now that we are trying to merge we know exactly what they feel. They've never wanted us and now we are a threat. Serves us right for wanting to be one of them. We have to stay together within and we've got to show them that we have as much right to be here as the pissed-off whites who've bullied their way into this country these last three hundred years. We've got to stay apart, stay together. That is the only way. . . . Ghettoes is right . . . look at Jews . . . only in ghetto can unity thrive . . . now they don't get pushed around any more. They are top of the world. (98)

Rajen rejects this and expresses: "Now that they [the Jews] are the tops, now that they are accepted and all that, do you see the writing on the wall? They are disintegrating, just melting into the sea of society." (98) As stated previously, multiculturalism as a state policy of Canada is a pretence. Rajen ridicules it:

> that's called multiculturalism out here. Each group stays together and once a year there's a three-ring circus, a zoo called Folkorama where everyone visits everyone else's cage. Hula, Calypso, bagpipes and all. Just wait for the mela. I'll take you around. (98)

The resolution of the conflicting views of Dilip (who professes attempt to assimilate) and Vithal (who prefers ghettoes) comes in a friend's speech:

> We've got to stand tall. And by God we shall. We shall build our temple at the confluence of the Red and Assiniboine and then we shall say Okay, we are ready to assimilate. Not here not now. Now it'll be bootlicking, applepolishing. (98-99)

Hence, the attempt to "try to assimilate" should follow "living in ghettoes." Another solution comes from Sridhar:

> Why does it have to be "them" and "us" all the time, why not just you and me, an individualistic approach; the best bet is to let time take its course, and come a couple of generations everything would be more even all around, within the community and outside; we'd have a lot more brown-white kids. (101-2)

IV

The last section of the paper is a concluding note which is an enumeration of Parameswaran's views on the Indo-Canadian Diaspora as comprehensible from the above study. Parameswaran's metaphor of 'Trishanku' illustrates the predicament of the Diasporic people: "Like the mythological king, Trishanku, they stood suspended between two worlds,/unable to enter either, making a heaven of their own." The members of the 'New Diaspora' go to the new land for material success but assimilate there partially and the feeling of nostalgia stays. The characters of Sharad and Savitri express this aspect.

The second-generation immigrants have problems of different nature. They do not have the vision of 'homeland' and 'past' in the same way as their parents have and identify themselves with the Canadians. While they do not identify themselves with the Indians, they are not accepted as Canadians which leads to anger and frustration. This anger and frustration is visible in the characters of Jayant and Vithal in the play. The second-generation women immigrants face additional problems. There is a discrepancy in the expectations of the society and the family from them. This dilemma gets conspicuous in Jyoti's character in the play.

The lives of the members of the Indo-Canadian Diaspora are marked by racism and the policy of Multiculturalism has not helped them to make their lives easier.

I would like to conclude with another observation that the agenda of Parameswaran's literary works including "Rootless but Green are the Boulevard Trees" apparently is to bring forth the complex issues associated with and the vast range of the experiences of the South-Asian-Canadian in Canada. Her works are political and voice a protest against the ill-treatment meted out to immigrants in foreign land. Although they may not appear as an enjoyable experience to the reader, the theoretical perspective indicated through her work makes them significant reading.

Works Cited

Hutcheon, Linda, and Marion Richmond, eds. *Other Solitudes: Canadian Multicultural Fictions*. Toronto: Oxford University Press, 1990.

Levinson, David, and Melvin Ember, ed. *Encyclopedia of Cultural Anthropology*. New York: Henry Holt, 1996.

Mishra, Vijay. "New Lamps for Old." *Interrogating Post-Colonialism: Theory, Text and Context*. Ed. Harish Trivedi and Meenakshi Mukherjee. Shimla: IIAS, 1996.

Parameswaran, Uma. "Rootless but Green are the Boulevard Trees." *Sons Must Die and Other Plays*. New Delhi: Prestige, 1998.

Parameswaran, Uma. *SACLIT: An Introduction to South-Asian-Canadian Literature*. Madras: East-West Books, 1996.

______. *Trishanku and Other Writings*. New Delhi: Prestige, 1998.

Payne, Michael, ed. *A Dictionary of Cultural and Critical Theory*. U.S.A.: Blackwell, 1996.

Rushdie, Salman. *Imaginary Homelands*. London: Granta, 1991.

Vassanji, M.G., ed. *A Meeting of Streams: South Asian Canadian Literature*. Toronto: TSAR, 1985.

______. *No New Land*. Toronto: Penguin, 1992.

Sending Roots: A Study of Uma Parameswaran's "Sita's Promise" and "Rootless but Green are the Boulevard Trees"

R. VEDAVALLI
Bharathi Women's College, Chennai

Our age is the age of migration and the Expatriate writer is 'the contemporary everyman.' Meenakshi Mukherjee has aptly commented on this situation in her 'Inside the Outsider': "Today it is not at all rare to find a writer for whom the multi-cultural situation is not only a subject matter but a mode of perception as well."

The process of acculturation is inevitability that cannot be escaped by an immigrant to a culture different from his or her own. The transplanted writers explore the immigrant experiences. Their works reflect their expatriate sensibility—the experience of alienation, nostalgia and transplantation—that they undergo during the process of acculturation and acclimatization. The present paper proposes to study the problems of the immigrants at various levels and their struggle between the pulls of two cultures by a study of Uma Parmeswaran's "Sita's Promise" and "Rootless but Green are the Boulevard Trees".

Uma Parameswaran born and educated in India is at present a professor of English at the University of Winnipeg and involved in the Indo-Canadian and Women's communities in Winnipeg. She is also a poet and playwright and a producer of weekly television shows on India and Indians in Canada, besides being a writer of a few critical essays.

Uma Parameswaran talks about four phases in the immigrant's life:

> The four phases are: first, wonder and fear at the new world around oneself and nostalgia for the world left behind; second an overrid-

> ing impulse to survive in the new world that makes one immerse oneself in one's profession or family, and often precludes political or social participation in the larger society; third, after one has found job security, a turning towards organizational activity within one's own ethnocentric community; and finally, an active participation in the larger political and social arena outside one's own immediate community.

Though Uma Parameswaran claims that most immigrants reach the final phase, the question remains whether complete assimilation is possible. According to the psychiatrist James Tyhurst, a merger into the cultural mainstream of the host nation is very difficult for the first generation. The fact remains that the immigrants, definitely the first generation, might acquire a relative adjustment, that is 'acculturation,' but not 'assimilation.' 'Acculturation' is the adoption of changes in external behaviour for a smoother acceptance by the new society, whereas 'the assimilation' is the ability to react instinctively and emotionally to a culture. The degree of assimilation is in direct proportion to the degree of friendly reception by the host country and the immigrant's experiences in the host country. It also depends on the age and the immigrant's length of stay in the two cultures. In the process of acculturation and assimilation, every immigrant has to unlearn what he has learnt in his own culture and undergo the learning process anew in the alien culture. The old order has to give way to new. This is expressed by Clarke Blaise as 'Unhousement' and 'Enhousement.' The process of transplantation is relatively easier for the younger generation immigrant who has not got his roots firmly fixed in the culture of his birth. All these problems and the various stages in the process of acculturation and assimilation are clearly portrayed by Uma Parameswaran in her plays "Sita's Promise" and "Rootless but Green are the Boulevard Trees."

The play "Sita's Promise" was written for the 'Arangetram' of the first graduates (Uma Parameswaran's daughter being one of them) who have undergone Bharatanatyam dance lessons in the town Winnipeg. The play links epic India with modern Canada through myth and dance. Uma Parameswaran states that the play "Sita's Promise" belongs to the first collective phase of Indo-Canadian experience, though in the personal chart, it falls on the third phase. "Sita's Promise" constitutes testimony to Uma Parameswaran's cultural rootedness. Perhaps the best way to survive the pressures of hybridity is to keep contact with one's roots.

"Rootless but Green are the Boulevard Trees" depicts real life like people in the Indo-Canadian community and the events, situations and experiences pictured are so common and typical that occur in various families of the immigrants in Canada. The play centers around an East Indian family living in the suburbs of Winnipeg. The characters of the play belong to three generations. The three generations represent the various stages and degrees of change in the marriages of two cultures by their appearance, language and values.

The parents, Sharad and Savitri Bhave, and Sharad's sister Veejala and her husband Anant Moghe represent one generation. These two households left India in their adult years after marriage, for different reasons. The Bhave and Moghe children, who are in their early twenties, represent the second generation. As they have spent half their life in India and second half in Canada, their traditions and values are a unique blend of the two. The youngest siblings in their adolescent years represent the third generation. These children, Krish Bhave, twelve, and Priti Moghe, ten, have never been to India and are exposed only to residual elements of Indian culture as expressed through food, clothing and language including the religious stories. They are deeply immersed in the culture of their peers in Canada.

Uma Parameswaran's description of these three generations of characters and the situations they are put in reveal how acculturation depends on the age of immigrant and his length of stay in the two cultures. Sharad Bhave, an atomic energy scientist in Trombay, India, had quit his job and now works in Canada as a real estate broker. Jyoti, his daughter pictures his plight in the following words:

> It couldn't have been easy for him to move out after he was thirty-five, and it is no bed of roses here, mowing the lawn and painting the house and hundred mechanical chores which were done by servants in the luxury of family back home.

His wife, Savitri, is a schoolteacher. She is more traditional than her husband. Her changing into saree inside the house, wearing kumkum, sitting next to the service window and looking after the needs of the family during the dining times—all go to prove that she is still dominated by the Indian culture. When she is worried about her daughter's late night arrivals, Sharad comforts her thus:

> Don't be a worrier Savi. She is a good girl, and Andre is a decent boy. He behaves just like one of us. So respectful. And he looks like us too with his black hair and eyes. Besides you shouldn't continue to live in the prudish world of our youth.

Savitri fights a tough battle and never allows herself any time to think about life in Canada and its inconsistencies. She strongly believes that 'we carry our god within us and with us wherever we go.'

Jyoti reminds Savitri of the comforts she has lost in leaving India.

Jyoti: If anything, you are the one who's got a bad deal. Granddad's house, now what a mansion, and here you are working your fingers to the bone, scrubbing and polishing (with sudden passion) I'll start hating this place the day your hands lose their softness.

Savitri: They will survive but they'll survive, but will our spirits? No matter how long we live here, it is never long enough to forget either our old ways or our old comforts.

Savitri is not worried about the loss of comforts. But she struggles to keep her spirit alive. She can't stand the idea of her spirit dried up in the cold of Canada. She is Indian in spirit. She is unable to cut herself off from Indian ethos and sensibility. In the core of her being, she still remains an Indian though she got acculturated to Canadian situation externally. For example, though she doesn't prevent her daughter Jyoti from dating as an Indian mother would have done, still she cannot allow the father to know the escapades of the daughter. So she deprives Jyoti of the usage of her father's car but allows her to use her own.

Sharad feels sorry for having left India. He values family ties more and is shocked when he comes to know that Veejala is going back home resigning her job and leaving the family.

> How could she? Without telling us anything at all. Why did I choose this godforsaken eternal winter of a place, except so we could foster a sense of family even though so far from home? Just to be near her so we'd have each other to turn to in time of need. But she never came, never asked for help. (62)

He couldn't imagine any other reason but some illicit relationship, being influenced by Canadian culture. 'Why else would any woman leave her husband and home? . . . At her age, too, gods, help us. She's crazy." (63) Savitri, more balanced than Sharad blames the environment for Sharad's such thoughts: "I wonder if we aren't being brainwashed by our environment?—that we can think only of illicit relationship at the root of all troubles." (63) But the real cause of Veejala's decision to leave Canada is racial and gender discrimination: "Asked if she felt she had been discriminated against because of her sex, Dr. Moghe said, 'I happen to be of the wrong colour as well.'" (65)

The first-generation immigrants suffer a lot before they can root themselves in the alien soil. They face tough competition and racial discrimination wherever they go. The idea of assimilation seems a far-fetched one, when the immigrants undergo such hardships. Many people, like Sharad, bear it silently for practical reasons, but some rebellious spirits like Veejala prefer to suffer in their own country than in the alien soil. Asked if conditions were any better in India, she said they were not, but she would feel better wasting her life in her native country than wasting it in the backwoods of Canada. (64)

For the first generation immigrants who have spent most of their life in India and have settled in Canada in their middle ages, the conflict is not so intense because their roots are still in India. They have their own country to fall back at any time. But the second generation suffers worse as they think Canada is their land and try to grow roots and get assimilated.

Jayant: Our people, our old country, Dad, there's no 'our people' and no 'old country' for anyone in the world anymore, least of all for us. This is our land and here we shall stay.

Sharad: Roots, son, roots. Can we really grow roots here?

Jayant: Sure Dad. (34)

Jayant is very hopeful of their survival in the alien soil. He compares the immigrants to the tall Ontario poplar trees that look evergreen and beautiful though planted in Manitoba. But Sharad reminds the truth that the one in their garden dried up and are told by their neighbour that they are not native to Manitoba and may dry up one winter just like that." Shared expresses his diffidence: "if an Ontario poplar can't grow and survive in Manitoba soil, what chance do we have?" (35)

Jayant and his friends are greatly disappointed when the truth dawns on them that the whites are not ready to accept them and consider them on equal terms.

> Assimilate, my ass. They don't want us to assimilate. They want us out. We'll be squashed like bugs soon. All these years we thought the isolation was coming from us, but now that we are trying to merge we know exactly what they feel. (51)

The host's unwillingness to treat the immigrants as equals, compels these people to give up their faith in assimilation and prevents them to surrender their ethnic identity, to merge with the cultural mainstream of their adopted country. In order to save himself from the psychological crisis of his identity, the immigrant is compelled to cling to his own traditions and to mix with his own people rather than suffer from total rootlessness and alienation from both the cultures. "Serves us right for wanting to try to be one of them. We have to stay separate from them and stay together within and we've got to show them that we have as much right to be here as the pissed-off whites. . . . We've got to stay apart, stay together. That's the only way." (51) Though Uma Parameswaran has categorized nostalgia as an element of the first phase, the very fact that one turns towards ethnocentric community organization goes to prove that the immigrant never gets over the feeling of 'nostalgia.'

Vithal, gives the example of Jews who ghettoised themselves and toughened, did everything five times better than others and are on top of the world. Now, they don't get pushed around any more. This goes to prove that if one has his roots strong in his culture, he can flourish anywhere. Uma Parameswaran gives more importance to family bondage and emotional ties between the family members, the core of Indian culture. Jayant's giving up his idea of going out, Jyoti's refusal to date with Andre, Priti being consoled by Jayant and the happy family gathering at the end of the play all go to prove not only Uma Parameswaran's cultural rootedness but the younger generation's strong footedness in their tradition. The immigrants hope to survive in the alien culture being nourished by the strength of family bondage. The third generation is protected from the trauma of cultural conflict by the protective care of the second generation. Krish and Priti are happy children not much torn by the cultural conflict.

The argument between Jayant, Vithal, Sridhar and others drives home the emptiness of Canada's loud declarations and claim to multiculturalism. 'They feel that assimilation is not an allegiance to the rational, mechanical, achievement-oriented western culture, adhering to whiteman's value system. Rather they expect Canada to become a melting pot where different people from different cultures and ideas co-exist on equal terms. Vithal says:

> We've to stand tall. And by God we shall. We shall build our temple at the confluence of the Red and Assiniboine and then we shall say Okay, we are ready to assimilate. Not here, not now. Now it'll be bootlicking, apple-polishing.

Uma Parameswaran envisages that "after a couple of generations everything would be more even all around, within the community and outside, we'd have a lot more brown-white kids and the problem." It is symbolically pointed out by the flourishing beautiful green boulevard trees though rootless they are. It is enough that it survives: "it is there and it is green, it is beautiful." (83)

NOTES

1. Viney Kirpal, *The Third World Novel of Expatriation* (New Delhi: Sterling, 1989).
2. P. Marudanayagam, "South Asian Diaspora in Canada: Uma Parameswaran's SACLIT," *Decolonisation and After:* Studies in Indian and Canadian Writings (New Delhi: Creative, 1999).
3. Uma Parameswaran, "Rootless but Green are the Boulevard Trees" and "Sita's Promise" in *Sons Must Die and Other Plays* (New Delhi: Prestige, 1997).

Cultural Issues in Uma Parameśwaran's "Dear Deedi, My Sister"

K. BALACHANDRAN
Annamalai University

Uma Parameswaran, born and educated in India, immigrated to Canada in the 1960s. Having established as a Professor of English at the University of Winnipeg, she has founded the PALI (Performing Arts and Literature of India). Her "Dear Deedi, My Sister" is a short play but the impression it leaves, is really big and powerful. Through it, she brings to light the multiculturalism, which is prevalent in Canada, and its effects on various immigrants.

"Dear Deedi, My Sister" was composed in the 1980s, though it was in draft form much earlier, as Uma Parameswaran says in the "Author's statement: First Person Singular."[1] As one who had served "on the Board of Immigrant Women's Association of Manitoba, and the Margaret Laurence Chair of Women's Studies," (11) she portrays the problems that ravaged the larger immigrant community in Canada.

The play won the first prize in *Caribe* Playwriting contest of 1989 and was published in *Caribe* (April 1990). The play is about the middle class people who immigrated to Canada from ten countries (i) India (ii) Nicaragua (iii) Kenya (iv) Philippines (v) Nigeria (vi) Pakistan (vii) Hong Kong (viii) Sri Lanka (ix) Japan and (x) Somalia, and they are represented by Sapna, Mariella, Wamahu, Ilago, Sekoni, Aziza, Choi Chan, Chandri, Yokio and Guuled and Sagal respectively. The place of action is the living room of Sapna's house in Winnipeg.

Sapna, an immigrant from India in her late twenties, is the main character who narrates everything to us. Her sister Deedi is in India. For a woman who has settled in a foreign country, it is natural to expect letters from her motherland. Sapna says, "When I first came, the mailman's daily visit was my lifeline." (63) Even though she is in Canada, her heart is still in India and with her relatives. Nature is "both bounteous and tyrannical" to her. (63) As in India, in Canada also wheat grows in "miles and miles of prairie gold." In the land around her, there are cedar and fir trees; but in the landscape of her memory, "there are other smells and sounds of mango blossoms, monsoon rains, and temple bells." (63) She has been longing to hear the temple bells which she used to hear in India; to inhale the smell of incense stickers which she used to burn for Lord Parameswaran; to see Lord Nataraja, the presiding deity of dance; to walk to the temple to have a glance of Lord Shiva. All these she describes to her elder sister, Deedi, who is far away in India. Yet the one thing she can now do is to dance before the presiding deity, Lord Nataraja.

Now we have the ten people from ten different countries. They are the immigrants to Canada. When each one speaks out his or her mind, we know what is the issue in Canada. The dramatist, Uma Parameswaran, has done a good job of allowing them to speak for her. As India is a land of many cultures, Canada too is a land of many cultures. Each one has his or her issue to face and deal with.

Mariella, a young woman from Nicaragua speaks out for her side. The beach road is broad where the polished tar flings mirages. The sand is stretched out and her feet lap Eternity. The blind beggar stares. She has spent, "wreck of thirty ruinous years/ When the sheep looked up and were not fed." (64) She says that she is pledged to the land which her love has made their home. Now we learn that anybody who immigrates to any country should consider the new country as his/her home.

Then, we listen to Wamahu, a young woman from Kenya. Anybody who is not a multilinguist has to face the language problem. Wamahu spells out, "I stand alone/Amid masks that speak an alien tongue." She longs to go to her native country.

> Far far those I loved and love
> And far the fragrance of my native flowers
> O'er which bees murmur homeland tunes. (64)

Now we meet a school-going boy Ilago from the Philippines. He sings songs in French in his school. He asks his mother whether she can change his name to Jim or David or something because they face racist discrimination. He has his own doubt, if his colour is changed, it would be nice.

> When the snow comes, Ma,
> I'll get less brown, won't I?
> It would be nice to be white,
> More like everyone else. (65)

Then, we meet Sekoni, a young man from Nigeria. He cannot understand or identify himself with others. So he asks,

> Who are these faceless people
> among whom my life is oozing away?

In turn they ask him "Why are you here?" Immigration can raise any number of issues and these are some of them.

When one lands on a foreign land, even food becomes an issue. One may not like the food which is available there. Some may develop indigestion too. Nayana, a young Gujarati woman, when she returns from the big street after buying vegetables, is shocked to see "animals hanging from hook/like we hang bananas" (66) and her stomach churns and she rushes out. Since she is a vegetarian, she cannot understand or stand to bear a scene like this. She later complains, "But it is hard for me to speak English." (66) For this, one is helpless. Before immigrating to any country, one should think about and see the prevalent conditions there.

Next, we see Aziza, an older woman from Pakistan. She complains to her son about the kind of place he has brought her to:

> Where the windows are always closed
> and the front door is always locked? (66)
> But I cannot breathe this stale *air*. (67)

She is thoroughly dissatisfied with the living conditions, where she does not have the freedom or has the fear even to open the windows or front door. About cooking also, her comments make us think:

> with yesterday's cooking smells
> going round and round.
> Son, cooking is an everyday thing
> not a Sunday work alone.
> And son, cooking should smell good. (67)

She can no more tolerate a prison-like atmosphere.

> Open the windows, son
> I am too used to the sounds
> of living things. (67)
> Open the windows, son,
> and let me go back
> to sun and air. (67)

Next, we meet Choi Chan, a middle aged man from Hong Kong who cannot find comfort in those thorny spruce and asks:

> Where's the fire that can sustain us
> In this alien land of endless skies?
> Where the friend who'll lend a hand
> So we stand tall in our own eyes? (68)

In a new land who can come to one's help? Can one call anybody as one's friend?

Now as a change, we meet the Indian, Sapna who describes the pitiable conditions in which one has to live. In Winnipeg, one cannot get servants for household chores. "They prefer to work in weaving mills, garment factories, construction sites." (68) The water level in the well is very low and an electric motor pump set cannot be installed. So, immigrant women have to spend more time in drawing water; because of that they have welts on their palms and they have shoulder-ache.

Next, we meet Chandri, a woman from Sri Lanka. She lists the issues one after another. Here people have apartments but they need more winter clothes. Bihari in his basement bachelor suite has driven himself to suicide. Azar's mother is homesick for windows. Latha is caught between love for her half-witted daughter and her egotistic husband. Her mind cannot tolerate these futile attempts.

Next, we see Yokio, a woman from Japan, who says that those who are unfit to see the light of day are dropped in a white-lid jar and thrown down the incinerator.

Again we listen to Sapna addressing her sister Deedi in India. Wherever we are, death is unavoidable—whether one is in one's motherland or in a foreign land. "But death, till now a distant stranger, knocked on our door last month, and we had to lay out one of our dearest friends." She says that their heart still yearns to touch the waters of the Ganga before it can go in peace to its eternal rest.

> "Gangajal," he said, "I need Gangajal to wash him." (71)

She took down a cup size copper pot to hand over. His hands were trembling as she placed it there and he died. Death brings people together

> We came together then, all of us,
> two hundred and more. (71)

The play at last has a chorus where all the above-mentioned speakers join.

> We are New Canadians
> Come from many races
> Black, White, Olive, Brown,
> All alike, for all the many places
> High tech, mid tech, no tech
> Are one. (72)

Their chorus tells us very many things.

> What we were not told, never guessed,
> Is written on our children's faces
> Furrowed with tears because of our race
> Or colour, or tongue that stumbles
> Over words so alien to the many places
> From which we've come. (73)

They see their young ones' faces

Slapped by unthinking scorn, unfeeling barbs,
From closed fists and closed hearts? (73)

Sapna, the main character, expresses her anguish to her sister, Deedi, that they must build their temple in Canada. "We must build our temple here, here where the Assiniboine flows into the Red. And we shall bring Ganga as Bhagiratha did of old." (73)

Though much action is not there in the play, many more ideas are there. They reveal the playwright's anguish and also her optimism that Canada's fields are sown with gold, their lives should be bright with golden sheaves of corn. A dream can come true if there is real understanding, love and give-and-take attitude. Hence, if the immigrants are ready to follow this, nothing can be an issue to them and anything can be solved amicably for a peaceful co-existence and harmony.

NOTE

1. Uma Parameswaran, *Sons Must Die and Other Plays* (New Delhi: Prestige, 1998).

The Ambivalent Note: A Critical Study of Uma Parameswaran's "Sons Must Die"

S. GANESAN
H.H. The Rajah's College, Pudukottai

'We are Earth's best, that learnt her lessons here.
Life is our cry. We have kept the faith!' we said;
'We shall go down with unreluctant tread
Rose—crowned into the darkness!'

Rupert Brooke, "The Hill"

War is not a civilized act. The human reaction to war has always been ambivalent. War has been extolled in some of the greatest classics of the world and, at the same time, decried by thinkers and writers like Bernard Shaw. Still, from time to time, countries resort to war to expand their territories and to protect their sovereignty. Here I would like to examine Uma Parameswaran's play, "Sons Must Die." It is set against the backdrop of Kashmir and the Indo-Pak War of 1947-48.

In this play, there are three mothers—Meenakshi, Zohra and Prem Behn—who come to Kashmir, from different parts of India, looking for their sons, who went to fight for the sake of safeguarding Kashmir from the enemies. Meenakshi and Zohra consider the fighting meaningless. According to Meenakshi, fighting is needless in the present context. For India has enough land; enough treasures to cherish and feel proud of. There is no need to spill the precious blood of young men for a dubious cause. (Remember, in the contemporary context, India, China and Pakistan spend millions to maintain their strategic points in the god-abandoned glaciers and mountains.) Meenakshi says:

Fighting for a region we need not have

Though ours by right it may be.
My country as it stands commands the sea,
Land, air, Oh why do they want more?
My India is wide enough, plenteous enough,
Rich enough, aye confused enough too
To want more. Enough have we of riches
Enough of troubles. We need no more, . . .
O what amounts we stake for this!
Lives, human lives, sons' lives, O India
Is this enchantress worth sons' lives? (17-18)

For Zohra, as long as the people of the land happen to be Muslims, there is no need of war; to her, it is the religion which matters and not the ruler. Hence she wants the war should not be fought. She says:

Happy is our land ruled by the learned and strong
And happy we so long as we stay within.
But new lands, why new lands? Why Kashmir?
People here are of our faith I know, . . .
What matters who rules them so long
As they bow to Islam? (19)

Prem Behn's perception differs from the other mothers. The geographical proximity of Kashmir has shaped her consciousness. Her admiration for the beauty of Kashmir, her feelings of patriotism and valour all make her feel that the fight for Kashmir is a just one. She is proud of her son, fighting for his country. She thunders:

Proud am I that my son is fighting
For such a prize. Lovely vale, had I a hundred sons
I'd send them all to fight for thee, and consider it
Scant sacrifice for such a treasure. (26)

Speaking of the sons, Meenakshi's son dies a 'satisfied young man,' having his childhood ambition of flying in a plane got fulfilled. Quoting his own words, "few men realize their dreams fully: few prayers are granted wholly." Like Yeats' Irish airman, it is almost with exaltation that from the tumult of the skies he looks down on the tumult of men on earth. His decision to volunteer, therefore, had, nothing to do with a sense of duty to them, nor has he sought glory and public acclamation by making a patriotic gesture.

Kishore, Prem Behn's son, at his dying moments, craves that his life may be spared. He wants do drink life to its lees; hence he is unwilling to die prematurely, much to the shock and amazement of his mother, who considers his outbursts unpatriotic. Kishore cries:

> I want to live;
> Feel the blood of youth coursing
> Through my veins,
> To race over the fields, to swim across the Sutlej,
> To see Spring's first sprig,
> To join harvest songs and dances,
> To get the sting of winter's freezing cold,
> To feel the sun upon my face. (32-33)

Kishore dies a broken young man, being unable to understand his mother, who wants him to accept his death calmly.

There are other characters too. There is a nun, we find her prejudiced against Muslims due to her past unpleasant experiences. She is not even ready to believe that they also can be good and religious. For, "the imprint of fear on the human heart is deep." (21) There is a dacoit, who is a cynic, at times uttering blasphemous words. When everyone is blaming him, he scores a point when he says:

> And so with one voice you dismiss me,
> You who so fanatically kill each other
> For your faiths, slaughter women and children
> Where I but steal their gold. (25)

Then there is a poet, a romantic turned disillusioned soul. He becomes the commentator of the nightmarish reality of Kashmir.

> Last night the moon was red. . . .
> The birds flew in from the east and said
> "The moon is red tonight."
> I looked up, and the sun was red,
> A blood red it was as it touched the horizon,

And where it touched, a red stream melted
And flowed down in blood. . . .
This morning when I went to the river
I saw them floating down with the current
Men-who-were rushing down the river
With frozen blood, eyes eaten away,
Limbs maimed. (19-20)

He is pained to see the sufferings of others, especially of mothers. In an act of extreme sympathy for the dying Kishore, he, in an emotional moment, stabs himself saying he may be taken and Kishore may be spared.

Thus, this play portrays the conflict between romantic idealism and the survival instinct. It portrays the sad reality of the loss of scores of human lives in an armed conflict. Uma Parameswaran herself admits in her preface: "the play deals with the pity of war." (8)

In the post-Kargil scenario, the play assumes special significance. In Kashmir and elsewhere, say in the North-East, Mother India is continuously losing her sons to war and terrorism. Both the slain and the slayer happen to be Indians or at least, the people of the Indian sub-continent. The play is pacifistic and prophetic in tone. It subtly advocates the need of finding alternatives to end the chronic conflicts which the country is facing now. Otherwise, the decree 'Sons Must Die' is here to stay.

NOTES

1. Uma Parameswaran, *Sons Must Die and Other Plays* (New Delhi: Prestige, 1998).
2. Rupert Brooke, *The Works of Rupert Brooke* (The Wordsworth Poetry Library, 1994).

Shauna Singh Baldwin

The Winner of Commonwealth Writers' Prize for *What the Body Remembers*

CSPSP, Jadavpur University*

Shauna Singh Baldwin was born in Montreal in 1962, is a second-generation Canadian and has technically never been Indian. Her parents emigrated to Canada, but she grew up in India. They returned to Delhi in 1971. She is the author of *English Lessons and Other Stories* (1996) and *What the Body Remembers* (1999). She has also co-authored *A Foreign Visitor's Survival Guide to America* (1992). Between 1991 and 1994, she was an independent radio producer hosting *Sunno*!, an "East-Indian-American" radio show. Several magazines have published her fiction, articles and poems: *The Writer*, *Calyx*, *Rosebud*, *Hum*, *India Currents*, and *Cream City Review* in the USA; *Saturday Night*, *Books in Canada*, *Prairie Fire*, *Canadian Forum*, *Fireweed*, and *McGill St. Magazine* in Canada; and *Manushi* in India. CBC Radio broadcasts stories from *English Lessons and Other Stories* on its prime-time shows, "Between the Covers" and "Morningside." Baldwin holds an MBA from Marquette University.

What the Body Remembers won the 2000 Commonwealth Writer's Prize for Canada and the Caribbean region. Baldwin also got the 1997 Canadian Literary Award for her short story, "Satya." "Jassie" won the 1995 Writer's Union of Canada Award for Short Prose.

---

* First published in *Readings*, ed. Sayantan Dasgupta (Jadavpur University, 2002). It is an analytic and exploratory volume of great significance and value, prepared under Canadian Studies Programme Students' Project by Arundhati Dutta, Debashree Dattaray, Ritam Dutta, Paramita Ghosh, Prothoma Ghosh, Sayantani Ghosh, Somdutta Samaddar, Payal Sengupta, Jaya Shroff.

English Lessons and Other Stories presents a wide array of experiences related to the Sikh Community-many of the stories are about relocation in an alien land. *What the Body Remembers* is the tale of Partition as experienced by two Sikh women, Roop and Satya, who are married to the same man. What links the two is Baldwin's ability to present public history through a focus primarily on the private sphere, her ability to tune in to the voices of individuals and synthesize them. Gender discrimination in the subcontinent is a major concern for her. Other concerns Baldwin enunciates are the patriarchal ideology of the family, the insecurities of people who have been uprooted (India to Canada and the USA in *English Lessons and Other Stories*, Lahore to Delhi in *What the Body Remembers*) and the privileging of the male child over the female. Baldwin is extremely readable; her language clearly carves out poignant images from the lives of her characters.

Shauna Singh Baldwin's treatment of displacement is sensitive. She does not portray Canada as unproblematised paradise. Her characters grapple with several conflicts, both psychological and otherwise. Baldwin is particularly successful in depicting the ambiguous identity pulls on the displaced/relocated. In "Devika," for instance, Ratan, on one hand, wants to retain his practices from home, and on the other hand, decides "Devika must wear a dress. And pantyhose, and no nose ring" (156) and "learn some Chinese and Italian dishes." (157)

Baldwin's concern for the girl child finds expression in the way she writes about the consolation messages sent to couples who have girls. Again, in "Lisa," Jaya warns Brenda, "Don't tell him it's a girl," (65) knowing that the father would reject a daughter. Sympathetic letters reach Neelu when she has a girl: "It was a girl, and there were telegrams and letters of sympathy from relatives." (139) A boy child is given priority when it comes to education, as in "The Cat who Cried." (127) In this story, though, the mother refuses to compromise on her daughter's education.

Cultural displacement, identity crisis and the conflict between adopting a "Canadian" identity (in terms of one's practices, dress, opinions, etc.) and holding on to one's older identities are important issues for Baldwin. In "Montreal 1962," (4) wearing the turban becomes the issue around which the complex claims of identity are played out. The turban signifies the difference between amnesia and memory, between anonymity and identity.

Baldwin's female characters are not silent sufferers. Against tremendous social pressures, they are locked in perpetual combat to lead their lives their way. Characters like Reena ("Gayatri"), Prem's unnamed wife ("The Cat who Cried") and the narrator of "English Lessons" are very much makers of their own destiny.

In their own way, Baldwin's women try to make the land which is not "theirs," a little closer to what they would identify as "home," by reproducing and replicating their traditions, stories, even lifestyles. The act of story-telling takes on an important dimension in Baldwin's *English Lessons*; writing from the perspective of these women is a way of giving them a voice, or rather, perhaps, of giving them an ear, for their eloquence was never in question. "Most of the stories in this collection are first-person narratives. Telling the tale gives the woman a voice, lets them break out of the silence they have been conditioned into, the solitude their silence has condemned them to." (Dasgupta, 35)

What the Body Remembers is an epic tale of Partition seen through the eyes of the Sikh community, and perhaps, just as importantly, through the eyes of a woman. The novel uses a vast canvas and concentrates on the period from 1928 to 1947. It evokes such important moments from public memory as the Jallianwala Bagh massacre. This Partition novel integrates a number of sensitive issues relating both to the public as well as the private domain, including the effervescing religious factionalism of the times.

It tells the story of Sardarji, the London-educated bureaucrat-engineer, and his two wives. Satya has borne no children. So, Sardarji takes a younger wife, Roop. As the country is torn apart by the events leading to the Partition, so is the family torn apart by the conflict between the women. In a way, the latter mirrors the conflicts of the public world. At the end of this novel, as in

Partition, there is no winner—everyone has made compromises on conscience, humanity and honesty; everyone is a loser.

The "Indian" element is very strong in the novel. The novel is set in undivided India. The author highlights the tragedy of Partition by uprooting her characters from their ancestral homes. Baldwin focuses extensively on the constant friction between the Hindus and the Muslims; she shows how Sikhs are caught in the land grab between the two communities.

The author makes frequent use of Urdu and Punjabi words. She uses words like "zamana" and "izzat." (96, 147) This is an attempt to "make alive" the characters. "They are human like you, and they are products of their time, place and environment, too," said Baldwin in an interview to Rick Rennicks on the Internet. But, Baldwin also seeks to see her use of language as part of the empire writing back. "The practice of italicizing non-English words," the author told Rick Rennicks, "are quaint hangovers from colonial times and should be dropped in our internet era."

Baldwin explores the man-woman power equation extensively; her stance is evidently feminist. She told *The Sunday Statesmen* (21 November 1999), "It's a very feminist novel. I'm a beneficiary of feminism." *What the Body Remembers* also explores the intricate relationship between women, Satya and Roop, their insecurities (Roop says, "I will be no trouble, I will be just like a younger sister" [16]), jealousies ("Satya wants to tear them from the girl's ears, watch as Roop's tender lobes elongate and rip apart, wants to take back what is hers, rightfully hers". [16]) and compromises ("then what is one more woman in a house where there are fifty people? And no other families have asked for me" [120]). The prologue highlights the author's con cern, "Against all odds, against every pandit's promise, despite a whole life of worship and expiation . . . I am again . . . born a woman." (11) The author effectively critiques gender conditioning and investigates the implication of "for-your-own-good," "what-will-people-say" and "the way-a-good-good-sweet-sweet-wife should." Shauna Singh Baldwin shows how Indian women are often treated as machines for production of an heir "who would carry forward the name of their ancestors." There is a clear demand for a male child. The prologue and the epilogue both emphasize how joyless the birth of a baby girl is. The author shows how to many of her characters being born as a girl is a fate worse than death. It is, to them, an inexorable "karma" that cannot be changed, come what may.

Women are expected to live by certain patriarchal codes regardless of their own needs and desires. Satya, the fearless woman who dared "not to lower her eyes before men," "pays the price" and has to share her husband with another woman.

The novel talks about the devaluation of women in marriage as baby-making machines, maltreatment of the girl child, animosity between co-wives, superstitions in society and the dowry problem. The novel ends with a telling epilogue (Satya's soliloquy): "I have come so far, I have borne so much pain and emptiness! But men have not changed." (474)

We asked Shauna Singh Baldwin over the Internet whether her novel had any connection with her personal experience, she replied, "Yes, and no: I began from my grandmother's story, but with the number of interviews and other women's experiences that became interwoven, Roop and Satya became composites, then became themselves." (Shauna Singh Baldwin in conversation with Jaya Shroff over the Internet)

Baldwin chose to write on such issues because she felt that the position of Sikh women at the time of Partition has not been explored sufficiently. Nor has Partition been substantially explored from the point of view of a Sikh in the writings of Indian writers, "diasporic" or otherwise, she says.

So, what is it that the body remembers? For Satya, the body remembers the pain and the sense of emptiness that come with being born a woman; for Roop, "what the body remembers" is often joyful, consisting of vignettes of her happy childhood at Pari Darwaza. However, she soon matures as a wife and mother, and "what her body remembers" is "what-women-are-for"—to produce babies for the husband.

Baldwin convincingly re-creates the colour and customs of colonial India in *What the Body Remembers*. It is a powerful novel, a moving portrait of a family in conflict and a nation in turmoil. Her collection of short stories captures a different time(s); but the issues, problems and conflicts her women characters grapple with do link her works together.

Works Cited

Shauna Singh Baldwin, *English Lessons and Other Stories* (New Delhi: HarperCollins, 1999).

Shauna Singh Baldwin, *What the Body Remembers* (New Delhi: HarperCollins, 1999).

Sayantan Dasgupta, "Silent Rebellions," *Indian Review of Books*, Vol. XIII, No. 10, Chennai: East West, July 16-August 15, 1999.

"It's My Job to Give Something Back," interview with Shauna Singh Baldwin, in "Impressions," *The Sunday Statesman*, 21 November 1999, p. 3.

A Sikh-Canadian View of Partition: Shauna Singh Baldwin's *What the Body Remembers*

MARY CONDE
University of London

In Urvashi Butalia's *The Other Side of Silence: Voices from the Partition of India*, a major source for *What the Body Remembers*, she comments, "*Partition*: the word itself is so inadequate."[1] Yet the term, made more sinister by its lack of a definite article, and by its connotation of a kind of scientific impartiality, has a terrible resonance, casting a dark shadow over the celebration of India's fifty years of independence in 1997. Even so, the Penguin book of Partition stories from Urdu, published in 1998, was given the title *An Epic Unwritten*. Butalia, who tells so many hitherto untold stories, finds it necessary to wrestle with the question, 'How important is it for us to excavate Partition memories?' and quotes the observation of Krishna Sobti, a writer and Partition refugee, that Partition is difficult to forget but dangerous to remember.[2]

Particular demands may be made of Partition narrative. For example, Shelley Feldman in her article 'Feminist Interruptions: The Silence of East Bengal in the Story of Partition' concludes: "the stories of Partition—of the pain, horror, and rape—need to be counterposed to other experiences of Partition, to the hope and opportunity promised by the creation of a Muslim state."[3] The danger of such a demand is that male stories of incorporation into a new nation may be celebrated at the expense of female stories of rape and abduction.[4]

It is Shauna Singh Baldwin's project to restore the woman's story, and she focuses on Partition through the twin concepts of women's bodies and memory, which coalesce in her rather curious title, *What the Body Remembers*. Since the name of one of the three main protagonists, Roop, means *body*, this title also suggests: what Roop remembers, but although a major section of the novel is devoted to Roop's viewpoint there is also much in it which Roop never knows and therefore cannot remember. Sometimes Baldwin attempts to make a virtue, narratively speaking, out of what Roop cannot remember, in a passage like this one:

> While [Roop and her sister Madani] have been at Bhai Takht Singh's, learning the Gurus' shabods and embroidery, so many events have passed them by. Mahatma Gandhi walked two hundred and forty miles to pick up a lump of salt and refused to pay the British tax on it. Freedom fighter Bhagat Singh climbed the gallows and swung for tossing a bomb into the legislative assembly to make the deaf hear; his Sikh friends and relatives say the Mahatma stood by as if he were deaf himself and, in the name of non-violence, just let the British kill him. The Mahatma raised the national flag of a free India and it did not have a strip of deep Sikh blue as he promised; across Punjab, Sikhs mutter the reason—the Mahatma doesn't care for meat-eaters. A famous pir gave a speech in Jhelum and he told Abu Ibrahim to give all of Pari Darvaza's donations at his mosque to the All-India Muslim League. Sikh demonstrators led by Master Tara Singh protested when the British gunned down Pathan Muslims in Peshawar; they were beaten senseless by the police just north of Pari Darvaza on the Grand Trunk Road. Now freedom fighter Subas Chandra Bose has been arrested for appealing to the Sikhs of Punjab to produce more men like Bhagat Singh, and has been deported to Europe. And foreign-made chunnis are still needed for burning, if independence is to be won.
>
> But Roop and Madani were in a school with walls twelve feet high, and all this passed them by.[5]

This passage does make connections between Roop and the outside world, through linking metaphorical with actual deafness, since Roop at this point has just become deaf in one ear as a result of typhoid fever, an actual deafness which also becomes metaphorical, since although Roop is taught that to listen is to obey, she later realizes, punning on *bad*, that

I have one bad ear that does not listen.
So sometimes, it cannot obey. (276)

But the main function of this passage is to disconnect Roop from any knowledge of, or investment in, outside events, and thereby to make a sharp division between what she, as a very self-absorbed young female, and (mostly male) others, might remember of these years. Baldwin's focus is not on the many Indian women, celebrated by Nehru,[6] who took an active part in the struggle for independence. The (presumed male) Sikh voices which say, and mutter, hostile things about Gandhi in the background also enable Baldwin to produce a multiple-viewpoint yet pro-Sikh novel. At least one review of the novel has criticized it as too hostile to Muslims, confirming Butalia's anxieties by observing that the novel's anger "bears witness to the sores that, fifty-two years after Partition, seem to be erupting on the body of a literature which—in the many masterworks that the cataclysm produced—prided itself on compassion and impartiality."[7] The passage also illustrates Baldwin's (or her editors') anxiety not only about the audience's sympathies, but knowledge, in, for example, its reference to *freedom fighter* Subas Chandra Bose. This audience appears to be perceived primarily as British, American, or Canadian, just as is the audience of (say) Arundhati Roy's *The God of Small Things*, and is a similarly Western-reader-friendly novel: Roop's elder sister, for example, explains to Roop, when she is a little girl, both the mechanics and the psychology of a Sikh wedding, so that this information is slipped discreetly to us.

What the body does remember, according to Baldwin, falls into two main categories, one of group memory transcending individual time, more usually seen as male, and one of individual memory confined to one lifetime, more usually seen as female, and a Western audience is likely to have more of a problem with the first. Baldwin writes, for example, of people moving across India, 'moving not in hope of freedom and independence, but from the fear their bodies remember from other ages.' (395) Roop's brother Jeevan says that he has discovered in the Army that it is not only, as the English believe, Sikhs, Gurkhas and

Marathas who can fight, 'but all men whose bodies remember humiliation and anger from this and past lives.' (174)

More conventional for a Western audience is the insistence on an individual bodily memory, transmitted without the help of the intellect. When Roop is forced to give up her first baby to her husband Sardarji's first wife Satya, she tells the little girl to remember the taste, smell and touch of her mother's body. (189) When she is forced to give up her second baby, she kisses the soles of his feet, so that when he is a man his body may remember 'the mark of this stolen moment.' (231) On her wedding night her vagina is a place the sixteen-year-old Roop's body does not remember owning, (158) but Baldwin suggests that it might remember, in giving birth a second time, that it had given birth before. (225)

Between the two categories of group memory and individual memory comes a category of group memory linked to individual memory through story, the story often transmitted via a woman. When Sardarji begins to fear the loyalties of his Muslim friend Rai Alam Khan, Baldwin asks,

> Does Rai Alam Khan think the Sikhs can survive under the Muslims again—the same who slaughtered and martyred their Gurus? Sardarji's body remembers life-preserving fear, passed down centuries in lori rhymes his mother sang him, in paintings displayed in the Golden Temple Museum in Amritsar, in poem and in story—though his mind is open, he assures Cunningham, open to his old friends like Rai Alam Khan. . . . What Rai Alam Khan's body remembers is a hundred years old, it comes from tales of domination by Sikhs. What his own body remembers comes from gory paintings of Gurus boiled and dismembered by order of Mughal emperors, the antique violence of Rai Alam Khan's forebears. These events, which are indelible, shape their karmic memory. (345-46)

The role of stories, whether in painting, poetry, or other oral narratives, then, is to consolidate a particular viewpoint; stories, it is observed elsewhere in the novel, 'are not told for the telling, stories are told for the teaching.' (336) When Roop's brother Jeevan tells her how he found his wife Kusum's body chopped up, her womb ripped out, 'his story enters Roop's body,' and this phrase conveys not only the horror of the listener, but the fact that the horror has become a kind of genetic inheritance: 'this telling is not for Roop, this telling is for Roop to tell his sons, and her sons.' (448) Roop's punning determination to 'remember Kusum's body, re-membered' (454) is nowhere substantiated in terms of a healing process.

Partition is also played out in terms of the dismemberment of a body: the cutting of 'a land in three, West Pakistan, India, and East Pakistan, like cutting arms from a body.' (387) This, of course, is a traditional image for Partition. A section of *The Other Side of Silence* is headed 'History is a Woman's Body,' and Butalia notes that "Mother India was imaged in feminine terms, as the mother, and Partition was seen as a violation of its body. One issue of the *Organiser* (August 14, 1947) had a front page illustration of Mother India, the map of the country, with a severed woman lying on it, one limb cut off and severed with Nehru holding the bloody knife responsible for doing the severing."[8]

In Bapsi Sidhwa's *Cracking India* (1991), a novel in which Partition is seen from the viewpoint of a Parsi child, the child expresses her feelings after witnessing a Muslim atrocity in Lahore by forcing her brother to help her rip a doll's female body apart.[9]

In one of Sidhwa's short stories, 'Defend Yourself Against Me' (1990), set in the United States, about the attempted reconciliation between two Sikh men and a Muslim woman who was the victim of Sikh violence at Partition, the narrator reflects in general terms on women as

> The fruits of victory in the unremitting chain of wars that is man's relentless history. The vulnerability of mothers, daughters, granddaughters, and their metamorphosis into possessions; living objects on whose soft bodies victors and losers alike vent their wrath, enact fantastic vendettas, celebrate victory.[10]

In Shiv K. Kumar's novel *A River with Three Banks: The Partition of India: Agony and Ecstasy* (1998) a male Hindu is offered the 'pick' of the young women on a train carrying Muslim refugees—when he replies '"Maybe some other day",' the chilling reply is: '"You'll be welcome any time."'[11] One of the celebrated Muslim writer Saadat Hasan Manto's Partition short stories, 'Losing Proposition,' first published in Urdu, is the more powerful in being completely non-specific. It runs in its entirety:

> The two friends finally picked out a girl from the dozen or so they had been shown. She cost forty-two rupees and they brought her to their place.
>
> One of them spent the night with her. 'What is your name?' he asked.
>
> When she told him, he was taken aback. 'But we were told you are the other religion.'
>
> 'They lied,' she replied.
>
> 'The bastards cheated us!' he screamed, 'selling us a girl who is one of us. I want our money refunded!'[12]

The conviction that no girl is 'one of us' as far as men are concerned is angrily expressed by a Muslim woman sheltering a Hindu girl in Jyotirmoyee Devi's *The River Churning: a Partition novel* (1967), first published in Bengali with a title which means 'The Woman Chapter in History,' who says to her sons,

> 'You want to partition the country, go ahead; you want to fight over it—do it by all means. But why don't you leave the women alone?'[13]

In Amrita Pritam's novel *The Skeleton* (1987), first published in Punjabi, Partition is seen by the female protagonist specifically as an offence against women:

> Hamida's ears burned with rage when she heard of the abduction of Hindu girls by Muslims and of Muslim girls by Hindus. Some had been forced into marriage, some murdered, some stripped and paraded naked in the streets.
>
> Thus passed August 15 of the year 1947.[14]

1947, seen by Baldwin too, in the tradition of these writers, as an assault by men on women, is not reached until about four-fifths of the way through *What the Body Remembers*; she expends much of her narrative energy up to that point establishing the special importance of bodies in her story. In the opening sequence, in which Satya jealously examines Roop, her husband's new young wife who is to bear him children, Roop's long hair, because it has few split ends, betrays the fact that it must have been cut at least once, so she is a new Sikh, (15) and her high cheekbones are evidence of inherited Afghan blood. (16) As a child, Roop has her body inscribed in the wrong language when the bangle-seller tattooes her name on her inside wrist in Urdu, (62) although it is this that saves her life years later at Partition when she is attacked by a Muslim gang. (427) At her wedding Roop deduces her husband's social status from his bare feet before she has seen his face: their pallor tells her that he only rarely goes barefoot, and a corn on his big toe that he wears European shoes all the time. (132) Roop, like Muslim and Hindu as well as Sikh girls, early learns to fear her own body, 'that lurer of lust from the eyes of unrelated men,' (112) and to fear sexual pleasure even in marriage. (208) Her body is denied both the food and the physical exercise freely available to her brother (32, 95, 113). As a woman, she must learn to read not only her baby's little body, (182) but to read all of her husband's body language—the twitch of a muscle, the lift of an eyebrow, the curl of a moustache, the flick of a wrist. (199) As she is deaf in one ear, she must also learn to read his lips, body language which Sardarji amusingly misinterprets as extravagant interest in his ideas, 'her eyes upon his mouth as if ropes of pearls fell from his lips.' (295) On becoming Sardarji's wife she must learn all his rules about her own body: that she must not wear a bindi on her forehead, vermilion powder in the parting of her hair, or a nose ring, and that she must clean her teeth with toothpaste and toothbrush. (163)

In some ways Satya, whose name means *truth*, is presented as a counterpart to Roop, and it is she who tries to downplay the importance of body by asking Sardarji, '"Can you tell now from looking at anyone's face today who is Muslim, who is Hindu?"' (257) Significantly, Satya dies before Partition, leaving Sardarji to cry 'loud and long as if his truth is gone from the world and only lies and pretences remain.' (330) Still more significantly, she has perished wilfully, by deliberately contracting tuberculosis; later, Sardarji, thinking both of his dead wife and of the terrible dilemma of Partition, reflects, 'A massacre by Muslims or slow death under the rule of Hindus—like choosing between cancer and tuberculosis.' (388) The stickiness of Satya's ashes as he sprinkles them into the Ganga becomes an expression of Sardarji's reluctance to part with the truth, but he does part with it.

Although Satya stands for truth and 'needs Roop for what Roop's body can do' (171) she is in no sense presented as bodiless. Just as Roop loses her early confidence in her own body through being completely subordinate to Sardarji, (199) so Satya's recovers its confidence once she has been abandoned by him: 'Satya's body remembers for her and it tells her to be daring in ways she could never contemplate before.' (298) In many ways their plight is similar: Satya, in being forced to let Roop eat the sweets she has made, grooved with the imprint of her own hands, betrays 'the work of her body into Roop's freshly hennaed hands,' (170) just as Roop is forced to betray the work of her body, her babies, into Satya's hands. This has its own parallel in Sardarji's being forced to yield his trophy, the boar he has killed, to the Englishman Farquharson, who claims it as his, (203) so that all three protagonists, as a representation of India, are robbed of what is rightfully theirs.

The partition of Sardarji between two wives is of course another way in which Baldwin plays out the Partition of India. The same extended metaphor is employed in Manju Kapur's *Difficult Daughters* (1998), a novel which Baldwin has identified as 'very different' from her own, perhaps not least because the second, young wife, Virmati, in *Difficult Daughters* is foregrounded at the expense of the professor whom she eventually marries and the wife whom she displaces. By contrast, Sardarji's second marriage results in a number of different, but equally important, pairings: Sardarji and Satya against Roop, since they have already had a long marriage when she arrives, and they are near intellectual equals, Sardarji and Roop against Satya, since they survive together, and together produce the children which she cannot, and Satya and Roop against Sardarji, two women who have been used by their husband to torture each other and who join together spiritually at Satya's death, as what 'Satya's body remembered has been felt for one long moment by Roop's.'[14] Roop immediately tries to forget this, to recover her own individual identity:

> But because Roop felt that one, single moment, that single solitary empathetic moment, Satya will live on in Roop, the way every older woman who uses a younger one is reincarnated in a betrayed young woman's body. Sister and sister they will truly be, the way they could never be while Satya was alive. Roop will be Satya's vessel, bearing Satya's anger, pride and ambition forward from this minute. She will contain her, woman within woman, hold her within. (331)

Part of this anger of Satya is directed against the British, about whom she has always told Sardarji unpleasant truths, for example that his promotion as an engineer has only been a sop to the ideas of Gandhi and Nehru. (163) After her death Sardarji thinks of the departure of the British as 'her Independence Day,' (389) and when Roop rejects the English names imposed on her children by the English governess Miss Barlow, she does so in the spirit of and with the behaviour of Satya, (380) showing how she has drawn strength from her.

Miss Barlow is a rather cardboard character, and the depiction of English characters generally is a weakness in the novel, one which tends to make one lose confidence in the depiction of Hindus, Muslims and Sikhs. It is true that there is a quite deliberate element of caricature in Sardarji's concept of England: his economically and idiosyncratically packaged memories of England are conveyed in his conviction that one return trip would be enough to cure his week-long bout of indigestion:

> 'One trip back to England—just one. A glimpse of Wordsworth's golden daffodils along Hampstead Heath, *Hamlet* at the Shaftesbury Theatre, a dinner with the dons at Balliol.' (301)

Sardarji's concept of England is also given invisible bodily form in the shape of his imaginary guide Cunningham, who routinely tells him the things that are 'simply not done.' Baldwin has said disarmingly that she had thought the idea was original, until she took a Pakistani friend to her writers' group, where she read a piece about Cunningham, and the friend turned and explained to the group, 'We all have one!' It occurs, for example, in Anita Panjwani Ahuja's novel *Flames of Fervour*, in which a Hindu character says to his son-in-law,

> 'We all carry on an internal dialogue. There is a white voice within each of us which keeps talking. Think about it. Whenever you are alone, what do you do?'[15]

However, Cunningham, a deliberately grotesque creation, is no more preposterous a figure than the boorish drunk Farquharson, or Miss Barlow, who, as she takes tea, says things like,

> 'Oh . . . there were massacres, yes. On my train. But I was titivating myself in my coupé and I didn't even know the train had been stopped and people slaughtered till I got to Delhi.' (434)

There is no English voice to utter even the ambivalent kind of self-criticism we find (for example) in Paul Scott's Lady Manners.[16] Perhaps Baldwin feels as Forster did when he was told by an Indian student that he was fair both to Hindus and Muslims in *A Passage to India*, but unfair to the British: Forster burst out laughing and said, "Well, of course, one *can't* be fair to *them*."[17] However, Baldwin's use of such crude stereotypes weakens the major passages in which she attacks the British, through conversations between Sardarji and Cunningham. The gist of these attacks is contained in a passage from *The Other Side of Silence*, in a real-life story within a story within a story. One of Butalia's main informants, Damyanti Sahgal, is telling of her desperate, impoverished wanderings through a landscape of terror. She is given unexpected charity at a resthouse, and one day the guardian of the resthouse appears and announces, "'I'll tell you a story.'" He says,

> 'The Englishman here, the deputy commissioner . . . he stayed in this rest house. I used to be his chaprasi. He came in one night and said to me, chaprasi, take off my shoes . . . I have shoes on my feet take them off. And today . . . I'll tell you a story . . . note it down

> with pen and paper . . . you know your baba Gandhi, he's given us a lot of trouble, a lot of trouble. That old man, he doesn't even stop for breath, he keeps telling us get out, get out. After all, where will we go? Here we are very happy. Baba, we'll leave because we have to, we'll leave, but not before we have taught him a lesson. We'll leave such a state of affairs that brother will fight brother, sister will fight sister, there will be killing and arson and rape, we'll leave such a state of affairs behind that he will not be able to control it, and he will raise his hands and plead with God to send us back . . . send them back. And then what will happen . . . his own men, his own people will hurl abuses at him, they will give him trouble, they will say look at this mess you have got us into. And he pulled out a paper and said, see, take it down, see today's date. I'm telling you we will go, we're not likely to stay now, but we'll teach him a lesson before going. This will happen, that will happen and everyone will say, Oh god, send them back.'[18]

There is no such convincingly sly, plaintive, prophetic, hectoring, genial, threatening, hateful English voice mediated through an Indian voice in Baldwin's novel, and I think it is a pity.

Despite this, one of the main strengths of the novel is Baldwin's ability to shift viewpoints. She is especially adroit at moving between the perceptions of Sardarji and his two mistreated wives. She does not make the mistake of making the man less of a character because she is arguing the case for women, and has said disarmingly in an interview that she actually identifies with him the most of the three, because he is ambitious and goal-oriented.[19] Her ability to shift viewpoints and the viewpoints of others is fascinatingly evident in a guidebook for foreign visitors to the United States which she published in 1992 with Marilyn M. Levine, in which she gives such advice as this:

> If you are from a country where it is assumed that signs are for the occasional stranger, and the signs are thus few and inaccurate, you will have to force yourself to read and trust the signs and notices that are posted everywhere. Because of the tremendous mobility of the U.S. population, everyone operates on the assumption that the written word is likely to be more accurate than information from a human being. Don't stop people to confirm information written on notices; you are likely to be referred back to the notice.[20]

This guidebook, or 'Survival Guide,' also includes the following observation:

> If you arrive over the Canadian border, you may be surprised to find that very little looks different. The length of vowels increases, the pace of life increases, but the landscape and standard of living look the same. The differences between Canada and the United States are subtle: most are caused by the difference in political and economic systems. The United States is a place of higher risk than Canada, with correspondingly greater monetary reward. (3)

English Lessons,[21] Shauna Singh Baldwin's prize-winning collection of short stories, has some of the same illuminating flashes of comparison as the *Survival Guide* (a young Pakistani notes that 'Americans have twenty names for the different kinds of donuts, more than they have for the relationships in their families' [53]), and many of the stories also deal directly with Canada, with what is called in one story 'pleasant, clean, safe, perhaps even boring Canada,' (119) as *What the Body Remembers* does not. 'Montreal 1962' was inspired by her own parents' experiences as immigrants.

'Toronto 1984' is the story of a girl working in Canada who must be 'not only myself, but . . . all of India and Pakistan and Bangladesh.' (65) She refuses to stand for a toast to the Queen who is the symbol of the empire her grandfathers fought against for independence. (63) 'Nothing Must Spoil This Visit' describes the relationship of the Sikh Arvind and his Canadian wife Janet, who refuses to understand why he lets himself be taken for a Hindu in Punjab; Arvind reflects sardonically that

> Somewhere between Montreal and Toronto, he'd given up arguing against her belief that people all over the world are the same, just with different languages, art and music. When they'd abandoned his turbans and left long arcs of his brown-black hair on the floor of a Greek barbershop in Montreal, a city become hostile to his English, hadn't she suppressed her French, ignoring Toronto's bilingual road signs? (103)

The analogies of the partition of 'pleasant, clean, safe, perhaps even boring Canada' are not explored further, however, except in

'Family Ties,' in which a (French) Canadian diplomat tells his Sikh friends in India that '"Quebec is like Pakistan, a place that needs to be cut apart from Canada as Pakistan was carved away from India."' (33) This story is mainly about a brother, the narrator's father, 'and his mad sister, partitioned by family ties,' (31) a young woman abducted and raped by a Muslim during Partition, and then repudiated by her family even after she has murdered her baby. It is an extremely bitter story, showing a deeply unhappy and divided family, and allowing no sympathy for anyone but the narrator and her betrayed aunt, the 'Moonlight Princess,' betrayed by men who value the group over the individual.

The contrasting shifting viewpoints in *What the Body Remembers* are managed partly by the repetition of key phrases in different contexts. For example, on the first page, when Satya jealously examines Roop, the young wife who has supplanted her, Roop's skin is described as 'smooth as a new apricot beckoning from the limb of a tall tree.' (15) Exactly the same phrase is used when we are introduced in flashback to Roop aged seven, (31) and when Roop fears that she may have lost her beauty through typhoid. (66) Satya's jealous perception is then later repeated again in the same words. (159) Similarly, a recurring image is of apricot buds sprouting from between Roop's legs, to be plucked by her husband and given to Satya. (25, 471) This imagery moves beyond personal relationship, for not only are Sardarji's apricots sorted by Satya to affirm his social status and the status of those who receive them, establishing his subservience to the British as well as his own eminence, but this sorting is used as a controlling simile for what happens after the cataclysm of Partition: 'Women and children are being sorted between the two countries like apricots brought in from the orchard.' (466)

Females in the novel are occasionally seen as emblematic of some movement, as when Sardarji thinks testily that Roop's behaviour in claiming her own children is just a symptom of the moral collapse of all India, (283) or Satya's infuriatingly slow servant is described as 'a non-cooperation movement of one,' (297) but Baldwin is more concerned to make a distinction between the individual female experience and the group male experience. Despite her very strong Sikh sympathies, she sees Partition more in terms of a male-female division than in terms of ethnicity or religion. Jeevan's wife, it emerges, was killed not by Muslims but his own father, who assumed that this was a better option for her than the possibility of rape. Her body was dismembered by Muslims after she was already dead, so that both living and dead she is subjected to violence both by those men who love her and those men who hate her—and the oppression of men is in Baldwin's novel mainly what the body remembers.

NOTES

1. Urvashi Butalia, *The Other Side of Silence: Voices from the Partition of India* (New Delhi: Penguin Books India, 1998), p. 360.
2. *Ibid.*, p. 357.
3. Shelley Feldman, 'Feminist Interruptions: The Silence of East Bengal in the Story of Partition,' *Interventions: International Journal of Postcolonial Studies*, Vol. 1, No. 2, 1999, p. 180.
4. Vazira Fazila-Yacoobali, 'A Rite of Passage: The Partition of History and the *Dawn* of Pakistan.' *Interventions: International Journal of Postcolonial Studies*, Vol. 1, No. 2, 1999, p. 9.
5. Shauna Singh Baldwin, *What the Body Remembers* (London, New York and Toronto: Doubleday, 1999), pp. 92-93.
6. Sitara Khan, *A Glimpse Through Purdah: Asian women—the myth and the reality* (Stoke on Trent: Trentham Books, 1999), p. 17.
7. Aamer Hussein, 'A partition of the truth.' (A review of *What the Body Remembers) Independent Weekend Review*, 25 September 1999, p. 4.
8. Butalia, p. 186.
9. Bapsi Sidhwa, *Cracking India* (Published as *Ice-Candy-Man*, London: Heinemann, 1991) (Minneapolis: Milkweed, 1991), p. 148
10. Bapsi Sidhwa, 'Defend Yourself Against Me,' ed. Sarah Lefanu and Stephen Hayward, *Colours of a new day: Writing for South Africa* (Ibadan: Spectrum, 1990), p. 350.
11. Kumar, pp. 99-100.
12. Saadat Hasan Manto, 'Losing Proposition.' *Mottled Dawn: Fifty Sketches and Stories of Partition*, trans. from the Urdu by Khalid Hasan (New Delhi: Penguin Books India, 1997), p. 198.

13. Jyotirmoyee Devi, *The River Churning: a Partition novel* (1967), trans. from the Bengali by Enakshi Chaterjee (New Delhi: Kali for Women, 1995), p. 13.
14. Amrita Pritam, *The Skeleton*, trans. from the Punjabi by Khushwant Singh (New Delhi: Sterling, 1987), p. 34.
15. Anita Panjwani Ahuja, *Flames of Fervour* (New Delhi: Har-Anand, 1996), p. 53.
16. Paul Scott, *The Jewel in the Crown* (London: Heineman, 1966), p. 475.
17. G.K. Das, 'A Passage to India: a Socio-historical Study,' ed. John Beer, *'A Passage to India': Essays in Interpretation* (London: Macmillan, 1985), p. 15.
18. Butalia, p. 119.
19. Mary Condé, Unpublished interview with Shauna Singh Baldwin, London, 30 September 1999, p. 6.
20. Shauna Singh Baldwin and Marilyn M. Levine, *A Foreign Visitor's Survival Guide to America* (Santa Fe, N M: John Muir, 1992), p. 4.
21. Shauna Singh Baldwin, *English Lessons and Other Stories* (Fredericton, N B: Goose Lane, 1999).

Anita Rau Badami

The Winner of Commonwealth Writers' Prize for *The Hero's Walk*

CSPSP, Jadavpur University*

Anita Rau Badami has been described as one of the newest writers in the field of Indian "sub-continental literature."[1] She has written two novels, *Tamarind Mem*[2] and *The Hero's Walk*.[3]

Anita Rau Badami was born in the town of Rourkela in Orissa, India. Her father worked as a mechanical engineer on the railroads. The job meant that the family had to relocate every two or three years. Badami, therefore, travelled extensively within India and this has enriched her works. She grew up with stories told by her extended family and it is often tempting to surmise that this story-telling tradition has worked itself into her works.

Tamarind Mem is easy to identify with Anita Rau Badami. As the author's life revolved around the railway colonies of India, so does this book. Like the author's father, Kamini's father, too, is a mechanical engineer for the Railways. The family around which *Tamarind Mem* revolves, too, moves frequently. The novel is a repository of numerous tales, the like of which Badami grew up with. In fact, one of the attractions of this novel is the way it catches the spell of so much of story telling. However, Badami refuses the term "autobiographical"[4] for her novel. She says she did begin writing this novel using memories of her past, but soon moved into the realm of fiction.

---

* First published in *Readings*, ed. Sayantan Dasgupta (Jadavpur University, 2002). It is an analytic and exploratory volume of great significance and value, prepared under Canadian Studies Programme Students' Project by Arundhati Dutta, Debashree Dattaray, Ritam Dutta, Paramita Ghosh, Prothoma Ghosh, Sayantani Ghosh, Somdutta Samaddar, Payal Sengupta, Jaya Shroff.

Tamarind Mem is a novel about the relationship between a mother and a daughter. The mother, Saroja, and the daughter, Kamini, have vastly differing memories and views about their past. *Tamarind Mem* shows how two people may have different recollections of the same past. In order to reinforce this idea, Anita Rau Badami divides the book into two parts: one focused on the daughter, and the other on the mother. The twin narrative is emphasized in other ways, too. For instance, the text is printed in two different fonts—regular Roman font for the narrative set in India, and italicized font for the narrative set in Vancouver, where Kamini lives.

However, there isn't any particular insight into Kamini's life in Vancouver, a fact that makes this setting a part of this portion of the narrative seem somewhat forced. There isn't really much to this italicized narrative than the telephonic conversation between Kamini and Saroja, or Kamini and Roopa, Kamini's younger sister. Though the telephonic conversations were indispensable for and inherent in the main narrative, yet one is tempted to muse whether this attempt to distinguish this part from the rest of the narrative serves any significant purpose in the novel or not. More specifically, how does it impinge on our location—does it offer any clues regarding the location of the narrator (in spatial as well in other forms), of the other characters, of the intended reader, and indeed of "South Asian Canadian" writers of the ilk of Anita Rau Badami? These are questions that may not be possible to answer within the scope of this essay, but they are questions, which, nevertheless, must be asked, if the essayists are to lay any claim to a legitimate location from/within which to read their objects of study. Perhaps, the author simply wanted to create the impression that the narrator is spatially situated outside India and is looking at "her" country from elsewhere. But, then, is it "her" country? In what way? To what extent? Is it meant to distinguish one who does not "belong" to the space one inhabits from those who do, and to highlight the dislocation of the former? But, surely, identity is too dynamic an entity, the relationship between geographical and experiential space too complex for us to imagine that these issues cm be negotiated in any fruitful manner so comfortably?

In the second novel, too, the twin narrative makes its appearance. One narrative is set in India and revolves round Sripathi Rao, his wife Nirmala, his widowed mother Ammayya, his deceased father Narsimha, his spinster sister Putti, his unemployed son Arun and memories of his daughter, Maya, all neatly housed within their "Big House" in Brahmin Street, Toturpuram. The other is set in Vancouver, and focuses on Maya, her husband Alan, their eight-year-old daughter, Nandana, and, of course, on Maya's memories of "home."

"This is a novel about missed opportunities—to reach out and try to understand people, to compromise," a reviewer of *The Hero's Walk* has written. Here, people end up craving "the power to reshape the past" only to find it is too late—tomorrow never comes. *The Hero's Walk* is, above all, a very human novel. If anyone remembers this novel, it will be for its sensitive treatment of stereotypes and their relationship with human emotions—arrogance, hurt, guilt, love and the inability to give expression to it.

The telephone was what connected the two worlds in *Tamarind Mem.* In *The Hero's Walk*, Nandana bridges the gulf between the two worlds. Badami uses the child's perspective to contour the two worlds—Vancouver (Canada) and India.

The idea of "home", as in India, fills Maya's heart, and Kamini's too, with nostalgia. "But, to Nandana, the idea of going to India is a source of great fear. For Nandana, "home" is, "250 Melfa Lane, Vancouver", BC, Canada, North America, The World," (16) just "a hop, a skip and a jump away" from Aunt Kiran's house, "put the house with the petunias that looked like a storybook picture, past the row of cherry trees without cherries and the small store that said Vancouver Buns, to the crossing where she would have to decide whether to turn right or left." (28) For Nandana's mother, Maya, "home" is miles away to the dusty, scorchy land, "where the road grew narrow and huts made of rags and tins and stolen bricks crowded around open drains," (56) or where "idlers clad in nothing other than striped and grimy underpants" continue to lounge "outside their huts, smoking beedis or gazing at the ground in despair," where women scrub on "listlessly at aluminium vessels around the tube well," spread out "ragged clothes to dry on flat stones beside the festering drain, next to the dusty roads," where little children (about Nandana's age or older) are to be found "squatted near the drain, next to the women drying clean clothes, grunting with concentration, their bums hanging over worm-ridden faces," where a certain complacent pot-bellied and hairy Balaji, the Canara Bank Manager, probes with his finger into his navel, nostril and left ear and examines his find with interest, standing outside "Big House", where "there was a mango tree in the backyard, a snake in a hole at the foot of the tree and a big fat frog near the well, but not a single ghost." (70-71)

Why is it so? Why does Maya, and so many who share her (dis)location, keep imagining, a "home" away from the world into which they have gone and made their homes? Is it because of some inherent sense of belonging that refuses to be forgotten? Is it perhaps evidence of a nostalgia that merely serves to highlight the organic relationship of the subject to the space s/he has moved away from? Is this lapse into remembrance of, even nostalgia for, the home lost, even for the unappetizing aspects of "home" meant to highlight the inherent goodness and sincerity of the subject? To reiterate his/her "Phir bhi dil hai Hindustani" credentials? Or, again, is it perhaps a flirtation with fantasy on the part of the "diasporic" author—is this imagining of "home" on the part of the character a way for the author to play out the fantasy of "return", if not in space then in imagination, to experience the pleasures of guilt and to finally arrive at a catharsis of that guilt?

Badami goes into minute realistic details, when it comes to India. Another characteristic feature of Badami's writing is her penchant for using "double words" in conversations between Indian characters. Both her novels are replete with such examples. For instance Ammayya, in conversation with Putti, says: "Chintamani told me that one should always watch the eyes. If they are yellow, then it is jaundice or some other liver trouble. If the skin inside the eye-lid is pale, it is leukemia. Mine is *too-too* red. My blood pressure is high that's why. I can feel it going *ghash-phash* in my veins, pet." (22, our italics) Other examples include *simply-simply, yes-yes, what-what, really-really* etc. Perhaps this is Badami's way of replicating the idiom of the languages we use in India; perhaps this is an attempt to stake a claim to authenticity by trying to catch the sound of a conversation in an Indian language within a work written in English—a language in which many of the characters probably do not speak.

Badami appears to present a rather depressing picture of her country of origin as compared to that of Canada. "Huts made of rags and tins," (56) "ragged clothes to dry on beside festering drains" (56) should serve to highlight our point. We, as Indians, have grown up with all this. But, it is unlikely that any of us would have ever looked at these either condescendingly, or, with fondness or nostalgia. Yes, they have been part and parcel of our lives, as have the lush green countryside, the cloud-encircled hills, the uniformed youngsters chattering their way to school, the lake near the movie hall which shimmers golden every morning—these not things Badami describes with equal enthusiasm.

But, perhaps, it is difficult for a writer in Badami's situation to do so. There is a tradition of describing India, as far as books written for a "Western" audience are concerned. The descriptions that have flowed off the pens of earlier authors have sometimes been dictated by what readers in North America and Europe have wanted to read, by the need to assimilate alterity into a more familiar space. Hence, India has remained, for many in the "West," a land of snake charmers, horse-drawn carts, elephant riders; a land run over with sick children, a country of dangerous pests and stinking drains. It is difficult to make a clean break with this tradition when one is writing for the same audience which works belonging to this tradition had cared to.

It is probably difficult for a "diasporic" writer to write about the recent urbanization, the sky-high buildings, the broad roads, the fleet of latest vehicle, the malls with their dazzling display and so on. That is not to say that these pictures of "opulence are more true than the others; to think so would be to indulge in self-delusion. The imported cars and shopping malls are, of course, deceptive—they indicate a different form of exploitation and inequality. They hide behind their flashiness the new balance sheet—a balance sheet that shows that access to a new imported brand of automobile for some comes at a certain cost to many more. The point here is, that when one only talks of the more easily discernible forms of poverty and uses images that have become cliched (even if that, too, is reality) and is silent about newer forms and disguises that deprivation and inequality, economic, social or political, assume, one's stance invites interrogation, one's intended readership and compromises made, if any, protestations of authenticity made, if any, to satisfy that readership, or otherwise, all become important to read.

One must say, though, that there are places where Anita Rau Badami does show an awareness of this very tradition of imagining India. However, to say that she goes as far as to critique it would probably be an exaggeration. Let us look at Badami's short story, "The Foreigners."[5] In this story, the voices of three people—those of Natalie, Edith and that of the narrator—stand out, and give us different ideas concerning India. "Natalie was always drunk. She drank to blot out the heat and the noise, the dust and the unending variety of insects and diseases, the subterranean hostility she could feel running like a tremor through the crowds of brown faces around her but could not see. She drank to the memory of a small island that she had left behind as a girl for a warm, moist country that made her feel nauseated and headachy more often than she cared to think about. Natalie, like so many before her, came as a young bride, married to a man who believed that he was working the mother lode here in this barely tolerable place, that he was on the path to fame and fortune." (95) This, we may observe, is India as it has been portrayed so often. In Edith's case, "She thought that anything was better than her world and India with its aura and romance and the unknown beckoned. . . . She was drawn to that distant land for much the same things that persuaded other immigrants to leave the familiar and embark on trips across uncharted waters—the desire for a new and better life, the belief that there was a fortune to be made elsewhere, the call of adventure." (95) This faintly fairytale-ish idea, too, is something we are fairly well acquainted with. The narrator's viewpoint here is quite different from the ones we come across in the other works of Badami. This viewpoint, we found more realistic, contemporary and easier to relate to: "Thin wisps of mist drifted away from the bulky domes of ancient palaces now partially obscured by a multistoreyed apartment building in which the lower flats had been occupied even though the building was incomplete. A lattice of iron girders still encased it like a cage and the topmost stories were empty shells with only outer walls and a few of the support walls inside." (97) There is also this phrase, which is ironical, yet, humour "whattodo sir, this is India." (97) Still, there are question marks. True, contemporary India has a lot of problems concerning religious matters, and, indeed "insignificant" acts, such as, Edith's bursting of firecrackers (and thereby angering a mob of Hindus against peaceful Muslims) are known to act as the proverbial flame in the keg of gunpowder. However, there will always be some who would find the situation trifle contrived, and the portrayal of the situation, laboured. However, it would probably not be justified (from our reading) to label this story a mere exercise in political correctness.

The question that remains, though, is this: does the sensitivity that compels one to write of the irrationality of problems like this back in the space that used to be "home" also serve to hide a silence, or at least, a lack of such an enthusiasm for portraying similar problems, in the adopted space? That is surely a question that we would like to see Badami emphatically answer in the negative through what she writes in future.

While Badami goes into minute details about India, Canada finds a much more sketchy mention in her works. In *Tamarind Mem,* the present finds Kamini in Canada, languishing far from home. The Canada we see is cold and icy, perhaps unwelcoming, but the mechanisms of this unfriendliness are never fully unveiled. More often than not, the unfriendliness of Canada is defined only in terms of its opposition to the friendliness and homeliness of India (that, in spite of the "apparent" unfriendliness of some of those who closet to the protagonist).

In *The Hero's Walk,* we get a glimpse of Canada through little Nandana's eyes. Her Canada is small, petty and simple. It is home. There are no complications and no complexities. One way of explaining this is, of course, by saying this is the point of view of a child, and therefore too many complications and complexities should not be expected. Still, this silence regarding Canada could be open to other interpretations. Badami has spent quite a few years in Canada and one may not be totally unjustified in expecting Canada to figure most extensively in her works. This may be a deliberate strategy on her part, or maybe a very simple case of unconscious omission. But it leaves her open to the question whether this omission is symptomatic of the presence of certain apparatuses in the adopted homeland that discourage the author from fixing her gaze on her new locale. Perhaps, then, the unwavering focus on India has to do not just with the fact that the intended reader in the "West" would probably want to read about India, more than s/he would, about Canada, but also with certain unstated prohibitions that may be at work even within the rubric of an official multicultural policy, or with certain states of mind evident in the displaced South Asian in Canada. Anita Rau Badami, then, may be taken to be a victim of such prohibitions and states of mind, when seen from the point of view of a reader who deems her guilty of this omission. In spite of that, Badami remains one of the most promising and readable Canadian writers of South Asian origin of her generation.

NOTES

1. As mentioned in an article on Badami, on the website, http://www.emory.edu/ENGLISH/Bahri/Badami.html. The phrase seems ambiguous to us. However, it seems symptomatic of some of the ways English-language writers of South Asian origin living abroad are posited, which is why we refer to it. This disjunction between our reception and the apparent satisfaction of those who wrote the text for and manage the website with the label, seems to us, to be the

result of a difference of location. We start with this sentence deliberately—to highlight once again that if we do Canadian literature, we would enjoy certain advantages and be in a position to stake some sort of a claim to relevance if we do its part of comparative literary activity with our realities being the focus of our attention. And this invokes not only the use of CL tools and the evident acceptance and employment of priorities associated with the CL movement in India, but also an interrogation of other stances vis-a-vis "Canadian Literature" which seem to be in conflict with our location.

2. Anita Rau Badami, *Tamarind Mem* (New Delhi: Penguin, 1996).
3. Anita Rau Badami, *The Hero's Walk* (London: Bloomsbury, 2001).
4. The website http://www.emory.edu/ENGLISH/Bahri/Badami.html
5. Anita Rau Badami, "The Foreigners" in Nurjehan Aziz ed., *Her Mother's Ashes 2: More Stories by South Asian Women in Canada & the United States* (Toronto: TSAR, 1998).

Diaspora and Beyond: Anita Rau Badami's *The Hero's Walk*

D.K. PABBY
R.L.A. College, University of Delhi

Three dictionary meanings of the word 'walk' as 'a particular station in life, sphere of activity, occupation etc.' or 'a mode of living' (now rare) and 'a manner of walking' seem to be relevant with reference to the title of Anita Rau Badami's novel. Each and every character in the novel is keen to carve out his or her own niche; and the effort seems to involve a 'heroism' of sorts. Even the writer seems to have made a refreshing and welcome departure from the flourishing tradition of novel-writing by a host of South Asian writers of the diaspora who seem to write for the NRI and of the NRI, about all of our angst over tradition and culture, and somewhat weary of our poor little rich people, political and social analyses of the lives they left behind and the new ones they have invented for themselves in alien lands. Fortunately, the book is not about the travails and tribulations of adjustment, assimilation and integration in an alien and somewhat inhospitable culture, except only tangentially. The life of the young absentee NRI protagonist Maya (Baker) who had initially gone to study abroad on a scholarship comes to an end right in the beginning of the book; and we are left with a young orphaned Canadian child Nandana who now occupies that space.

The embattled protagonist of Badami's novel, Sripathi Rao, a 57-year old advertising copywriter, though a diffident patriarch in the crumbling Big House, once a landmark of the Brahmin Street, perceives much 'heroism' in Maya having won the scholarship on her own. When his wife Nirmala expresses some reservation saying: "This scholarship and all is fine, but more important is marriage," Sripathi does not agree. It seems through Maya's potential success in the medical profession, he feels that 'at least she would be fulfilling a part of the destiny that his mother Ammayya had envisioned for him.' He hoped that the ancient disappointment he had inflicted on his mother would be lessened by his daughter's achievements. But in spite of all her brilliance in studies, Sripathi Rao had felt betrayed and cheated when Maya broke her engagement with her fiancée Prakash to marry a fellow Ph.D. Canadian Alan Baker. Angry and humiliated, Sripathi, who had sacrificed so many passions (including the offer of a journalist's job in the capital city of Delhi) to family obligations, refused to allow Maya to return to India for an Indian wedding and then abandoned her completely.

Badami says she wanted to explore the notion of heroism ranging from the epic mythological heroes who are 'so large, so enormous and so endowed with wisdom and bravery and goodness' to the Indian movie hero 'who is also larger than life, completely unbelievable, almost a cardboard character.' "These heroes occupy the Indian imagination so much," she says, "and then there is the fact that each one of us, you and me included, is heroic in simply seeking to traverse life from birth to death. We carry so much of hope in us, and our hopes aren't always realized."

Then the question arises: who then in *The Hero's Walk* is the hero? According to Badami: "All of them. Everyone, there is something about their lives that is tragic and comic and humorous and also heroic." In Indian dance, which Nirmala has undertaken to teach to the children of the neighbourhood, there's a 'hero's walk' and 'a villain's walk'—with a few different flourishes. "We walk that fine line between being completely good, completely bad and completely stupid." The book is chiefly about Sripathi Rao, his wife Nirmala and their families, as it intricately traces the lives of 'ordinary' Brahmins of a small town Toturpuram in Tamilnadu. The times are post-Independence times of manipulative political and social transformations in power structures in Southern India, the resultant shifts in individual values, expectations and lifestyles. In the first half of the gripping narrative, there is definite tone of irony, of humour, of wryness, of an interwoven and sympathetic understanding—especially after the bolt from the blue like news of the death of Maya and her husband in a car crash in Canada; and the necessity of bringing back to India Nandana, their only child, whose entry was earlier banned by Sripathi Rao. This tone is almost absent in the second half of the book except when Sripathi has to deal with the trauma of bringing Nandana back as he is the only legal guardian and trustee for her. Even otherwise, as family head, he is the one who must travel to Canada to collect the reluctant, confused girl as there are no known relatives on her father's side; and Aunt Kiran and Uncle Sunny, however much concerned they may be, are not prepared to undertake the responsibility of a young traumatized child. Bitten with remorse and guilt, he asks himself: "How can I face my grandchild when I am responsible for her mother's death." The more he thinks about his stubborn actions 8-9 years ago, the more convinced he becomes that his anger had somehow brought about Maya's demise. He had cursed her for her refusal to marry Prakash, "for humiliating him . . . for blacking the family name in the entire town. And the curse had killed her."

It is quite clear that Sripathi's palpable remorse makes Nandana even more distressed about leaving her home and flying across the globe. The plane and train journey from the Pacific shore to the coast of the Bay of Bengal is a wretched trial for each of them. Like the rest of her newly discovered and seemingly bizarre foreign family, she retracts to fancy, a daydream she has harboured ever since she learned about the death of her parents. Nandana finds life in Toturpuram uncomfortable and scary. She runs away several times, planning to fly to her parents and their orderly safe Canadian life. When the child is returned to the house on Brahmin Street, she maintains protest through muteness, as if speaking to the Raos or her teachers and classmates would break the spell of her parents' survival.

One day, Sripathi argues with his wife Nirmala that Ravana, not Rama, is the real hero of ancient times. Nirmala disagrees. 'A hero is humble,' she declares. Even Nandana is described as a heroine after she boldly accepts the dare of her new little friends and enters a dark tunnel. It seems, ultimately, Badami's novel celebrates daily heroism: Nirmala's tolerance in spite of all her protests and arguments; Putti's optimism about a late marriage and that too to Gopala, the vagabondish son of the neighbouring milkseller; Arun's political and environmental commitments; Ammayya's cranky survival with all the fears surrounding her of thieves; and finally Sripathi Rao's 'spiritual' or 'existential' growth as he accepts his own and other people's foibles. Little Nandana becomes an agent of light and incremental change in this shadowed household. When she disappears for a very long time, each person is forced to examine her or his role in the family. They do not want to lose Nandana as they had lost Maya, but how can they avert tragedy? However, the reader cannot always understand, empathize or fully enter into the consciousness of most of the characters especially the minor ones who possess a lot of scope of psychological development. The reader thus becomes more of an observer rather than a participant; to an extent it may have been done with authorial irony and distancing, but it does rob the book of its emotional effect especially in the later half.

However, the writing in the book is overall excellent as Badami has a good and sensitive ear for the local rhythms and dialectical variations of language. While clearly it works to place Sripathi and Nirmala as products of a particular kind of colonial education and ethos, it sits more uneasily on their son Arun, for example. The book captures in a most effective narrative style, using flashback, history and memory with an imaginative eye, the work culture, the general environs of a small town, of the shifting changes in times and values, etc. But most importantly, the book argues for us to consider that it is not simply the conflicts between the East and the West that are striking, but the conflicts within ourselves and our own evolving traditions. Its worth lies in the fact that even as a work of fiction, it does provoke thought and it asks us to examine the role of psychological dramas within our own families, our own communities, and our time in shaping us as individuals and as groups. Portraying her characters together in a series of believable climaxes, she has concluded the book with a delicately crafted epilogue. Here and throughout the novel, her writing is lively, honest, psychologically astute. *The Hero's Walk* is sustained by clear-eyed hopefulness born of a generous spirit and seasoned common sense; and I like to conclude my paper with Badami's own observation: "I find it touchingly heroic to just see people living from the day they are born until the day they die, so full of hope. You just wake up every morning and expect the next day to go well. And I find that touching. I wanted to work with that idea: the notion of heroism. And I think that's basically what the book is about." Yes, Ms. Badami, this is the strength of our ancient prudence and cultural heritage.

A Memsahib Reads India: The Fiction of Sara Jeannette Duncan

VIMAL DHAWAN
A.R.S.D. College, University of Delhi

Sara Jeannette Duncan, born in 1861 in Brantford, Ontario, was a rare woman of her times. Refusing the respectable, socially acceptable but hardly stimulating career of a teacher, she became the first Canadian woman to work in the editorial department of *Toronto Globe*, a leading Canadian newspaper, thus breaking into the male bastion of journalism. She had the daring to go round the world the wrong way, just with one female companion: preferred to enjoy the thrill of a train journey sitting on the cow-catcher in front of the engine in place of the comfort of cushioned seats of a compartment. A woman full of zest and verve for life. The spirit of daring and adventure perhaps made her aware of the limitations of a provincial society: she married an Englishman, Everard Cotes (Curator of the Calcutta museum) and left Canada to settle in India in December 1890.

Till it got Confederation status in 1867, Canada was a British colony. Since the majority of the early settlers were of British origin, English-Canadian literature, culture and outlook banked heavily on British themes, customs and concerns. The new reality could not erase the colonial mentality. Duncan, being a woman and a colonial, was conscious of a feeling of deprivation and a sense of marginalization. The movement from the margin to the centre is a pervasive colonial trait, a dream of every colonial. Duncan's decision to marry an Englishman was perhaps a conscious step of getting away from the periphery. In one move, she became a Britisher and moved to the centre of the empire. Marriage thus became a tool for engineering social rise both in her life as well as in her works. In her first short visit to India during her world tour, she had seen the grandeur of the Raj. She perhaps became enamoured of its privileges and prospects and decided to partake of these on a permanent basis.

While in Canada, her writing career was confined only to journalism: all her novels were written abroad, either in India or in England. Only two of her novels deal with Canada; her major literary effort can be placed in the category of Anglo-Indian writing i.e., the writing of the British in India. Several Canadian critics have concluded that one novel set in Canada and another having a Canadian theme is not really sufficient to call a writer Canadian, though she may have been born in Canada. Misao Dean[1] takes cudgels on behalf of Duncan when she states that Canadian literature should not be defined by setting alone, but by the author's 'viewpoint.' Duncan's willingness to see the Canadian personality as the norm, maintains Dean, certainly makes her a part of the Canadian literary tradition. In her two Canadian novels *The Imperialist* and *Cousin Cinderella*, she projects the Canadian personality to be not only different from that of the British, but also as superior to it. If we accept this as the norm, then Duncan failed to project this norm in her Anglo-Indian writings where such distinctness or Canadianness is made subservient to the demands of the Anglo-Indian discourse.

When Duncan came to India, a powerful colonial discourse was already in existence. She easily succumbed to the pressures of such a discourse which adversely affected her art. From being a balanced, objective and realistic writer of the Canadian scene, she became a biased. subjective and stereotypical Anglo-Indian writer. Her aesthetic honesty gave way to pre-conceived notions. As a result, whereas her two Canadian novels *The Imperialist* and *Cousin Cinderella* are considered masterpieces of craftsmanship, clarity of observation and objectivity of delineation, her Anglo-Indian novels are a mixture of stereotype and melodrama. Confusion in plot construction and inconsistency in characterization replace vision and imagination.

The Anglo-Indian discourse was a product of the Indo-British encounter, its high and low points, its hopes and despairs.

A large part of this literature, which consists of memoirs, reminiscences, travelogues, commentaries, short stories and novels was written by British officers, their wives and visitors. These people were neither keen observers nor did they possess sensitive perceptions. Thus, what we get is a one-sided picture of the times—full of cliches, preconceived notions, stereotype images, a set system of belief, retrograde ideas and home-cooked philosophies. These people and their writings are products of their culture and politics, which was a natural corollary of the western consciousness and the importance attributed to its centrality in the scheme of things. Said in *Orientalism* maintains: "Too often literature and culture are presumed to be politically, even historically innocent it has regularly seemed otherwise to me."[2] As a consequence, the picture frame is full of Britishers: Indians barely make their presence felt. And when the Britishers do notice Indians, they look at them through coloured glasses—glasses coloured by prejudice, a sense of superiority and a notion of being privileged. An offshoot of this attitude was that Indians were looked down upon. Such delusions, says Parry,[3] aborted discovery, encouraged generalizations, nullified the value of truth and precluded an appreciation of what could just be 'different,' not necessarily inferior. The Indians were viewed as a degenerated people, with a decaying culture. Justifiably, a reforming impulse then became a very important part of the British creed.

The Simple Adventures of a Memsahib[4] documents Duncan's early personal experiences when she came to India as a bride. The novel is very close to being Duncan's autobiography. In an interview she gave to G.B. Burgin,[5] Duncan admitted that it was her house, her garden and her neighbours she had described in the book. The two female characters in the novels—Mrs. Browne, the young British bride just arrived in India and Mrs. MacIntyre, the mature narrator—are two aspects of Duncan herself. Mrs. Browne's early experience, her wedding, her attempts to come to terms with the strange and rigid Anglo-Indian society reflect Duncan's own experiences. The novel is a sharp criticism of the life-style of Anglo-Indians, their hypocrisy and snobbery, parochialism and dullness. Frank Birbalsingh[6] comments: "The author seems less concerned with analyzing the actual—psychological and intellectual—effect of India upon her heroine than with providing factual information about routine, everyday, aspects of Anglo-Indian society." (71)

The Memsahib is set in Calcutta, as *The Imperialist* was set in Elgin. We find Duncan's consciousness vertically divided in the description of these two places. Elgin is a happy place where people are debating the imperial question. Elgin shows a rare degree of maturity, foresight and confidence in its independent judgement, while Calcutta is a hellhole, where the existence, the very survival of the Anglo-Indians is a big question. "This country isn't fit for a Christian to live in" (298); India is a "land of regrets" (306); these two sample observations in *The Memsahib* show not only Duncan's but the average Anglo-Indian's feelings about India. In *The Imperialist*, Duncan belonged to a 'colonized' here. The hope that her belonging to a colonized society might make her empathize with India does not materialize. Her observations, reactions and descriptions mark her to be a mere Anglo-Indian.

Dennis Kincaid,[7] a social historian, has observed that India had a curious effect on the Britishers or the Europeans—it either attracted or repelled them. Duncan on her first visit to India, was overwhelmed and excited by the exotic India. However, as she settled down in India, her reaction and observations became typically Anglo-Indian. In India, the Whites become immediately conscious of their superiority, that they were the members of a dominant race. England's prestige was great and had to remain so if it was to continue to claim respect and obedience from the natives. This could be achieved by maintaining certain distance from the Indians; thus Indians become second class citizens in their own country. The opening of the Suez Canal in 1869 drastically reduced travelling time between India and England. This resulted in British women coming to India in large members, and the era of the memsahibs began. One major consequence of the emergence of the Memsahib on the Indian scene was a new barrier between the Sahibs and the Indians. The lack of sensitivity and objectivity while delineating Indians that one encounters in the novel places Duncan firmly in the category of the memsahibs.

The Browns did not have much social intercourse with the Indians and Helen's only link with the natives was through her servants. To her, native servants are all cheats, especially the Bawarchi. It is so convenient to use generalizations and cliches to describe Indians that there is no further need of any real analysis. The description of Browne's Syce and the Pony, though ironic, makes one wonder at Duncan's lack of consideration for the Indians:

> The same roof sheltered both of these creatures of service (The Syce and the Pony), a thatched one; but between them a primitive partition went halfway up. On one side of this the pony was tethered and enjoyed the luxuries of his dependence, on the other the syce lived in freedom, but did not fare so well. The Pony's expenses were quite five times as heavy. His food cost more, his cloths cost inert, his medical attendance cost more, to say nothing of his requiring a valet. *He was much the more valuable animal of the two*, though the other is popularly believed in England to have a soul (88, emphasis added).

The callous indifference shown towards the Syce, a human being, is symptomatic of Duncan's attitude towards Indians who are less valuable than the animals owned by the British masters. Between the two "animals"—the Indian and the pony—the latter is better than the former. This highly prejudiced view treating human beings worse than animals shows a dehumanized Duncan, the typical colonial. Margaret Laurence, on the contrary, accepts colonialism as an opportunity to understand the human predicament. Unlike Duncan, she tried to understand the predicament of the Africans. She looked at them as human beings. Duncan, however, plays the role of a colonizer to the hilt. The natives for her are savages, 'things' or possessions. All references to them are derogatory. For example, Indians are routinely compared with animals and each description invariably mentions the colour of the skin. The 'Khansama' is brown and reminds one of a goat; brown people co-exist with crows and vultures; brown villagers die like animals and their servants are likened to cockroaches moving noiselessly to their holes. It is perhaps ironic that the white couple is named 'Browne' only the little 'e' distinguishing them from the 'other' despicable browns of the Indians variety.

In this novel, Duncan is more obsessed with the British and the Anglo-Indians rather than with the Indians. The first two chapters are set in England and the picture that emerges of the British women is hardly complementary. One gets a Jane Austenian kind of a glimpse of the British women's social life and attitudes. They are shown to be naive, ignorant and frivolous. Still, when compared to the Indian characters, they are portrayed as far superior and more intelligent.

However, Duncan is sarcastic about the rigid social life the Britishers had adopted in India. As long as there is no comparison between the Indians and the British, Duncan can afford to be critical of the latter. The Anglo-Indian social structure was based on hierarchy—first of money and then of position. When people don't call on the new bride Helen, her husband points out that Calcutta society bows to five hundred a month (that is his salary) but it doesn't hurry about calling. There are many people with superior claims—fifteen hundred, three thousand a month. Mr. Browne explains:

> The valuation of people is done by the Government. Most people arrive here invoiced at so much . . . they are always kept carefully ticketed and published, and Calcutta accepts or rejects them, religiously and gracefully at their market rates. (106)

Anglo-India is a totally mercenary society and Duncan suggests ironically that it simplifies living and removes complexities about social expectations and obligations. To a caste-conscious India, the class conscious Anglo-Indian makes a precise parallel. As the Hindu society was divided along caste lines—Brahmin, Kshatriya, Vaishya, and Shudra, the Anglo-Indian society was similarly divided into four categories. First in hierarchy stood civil servants and administrators (Brahmins); the British Army came next (Kshatriyas) followed by Businessmen (Vaishyas). The Eurasians (Shudra) stood at the bottom of the line.

Compared to the Anglo-Indian life-style at the turn of the nineteenth century, the Hindu caste system makes sense, as it is not based on the narrow considerations of money. The stagnation of Anglo-Indian life is aptly described by Duncan. The British social whirl, "the current that clung. every year and yet is always the same of English life in India. The old, old ambitions, the stereotyped political aims, the worn competitions, thc social appraisements" (129)—everything being done repeatedly ad nauseum! It is a sad commentary on the directionless and purposeless existence of the British in India. Referring to the sad reality behind the glittering facade of Anglo-India, the narrator comments: "If only the glamour of India left people with eyes to see." (129) The suffering, the pangs, the sacrifice, the isolation is all brought out.

The Anglo-Indian society had become very cynical about its position in India, which was made more vulnerable as the British perception of India in England differed from the Anglo-Indian perception of the Indian reality. The Anglo-Indians were gripped by a sense of insecurity: they felt trapped—they neither belonged to England nor to India. They had become so paranoid about their existence that any criticism of their functioning would force them to close ranks and present a passionate defence of their actions and attitudes. Duncan very quickly became one of them. Though she satirizes the hypocrisy and snobbery of the social pretensions of the Anglo-Indian community, she believes in the civilizing mission of the Anglo-Saxon race. While explaining Duncan's attitude, Woodcock writes that besides being critical of the rigid social structures of the Anglo-Indian community, she disliked the Bengali 'baboos' as they had received partial education in the English manners and belonged to neither the Western nor the traditional Indian culture. For her, Indian princes are fit material for comedy and when she portrays an Indian character convincingly and in depth, he usually turns out to be something of a villain. An example of this type is Ganendra Thakore in *The Burnt Offering*. Woodcock further adds that almost everything that Duncan wrote about India spoke well of those Anglo-Indian idealists who saw themselves as the carriers of the Whiteman's burden. They offered the Indians, despite their ungrateful opposition, the way to a more healthy and industrious life. (217)

Just how touchy were the Anglo-Indians about any interference from Britain in their affairs is characterized in Duncan's portrait of the "Globe trotter" British M.P., Mr. Batcham. "It was native India that he came to see and report upon." (172) Duncan plays upon the amount of ignorance that the usual globe trotting MPs show about India. She is very ironic about his concern for the Indians and paints him as a silly nincompoop who has no business to question the Auctioning of the Anglo-Indian Administration. Mr. Batcham is presented before us as an example of those ignorant Britishers who come to India with fixated, stereotypical notions, and who exemplify what Edward Said calls the 'textual attitude,' i.e. reality as visualized from a bookish angle. The Anglo-Indians hated such interfering lot as they wielded enough power in England to alter the rules and laws which could make life more difficult for the Anglo-Indians. Batcham becomes a prototype for another Globe trotter, Vulcan Mills M.P. whom Duncan portrays similarly in her Anglo-Indian novel, *The Burnt Offering*. Like Mills, Batcham is all for the freedom of the Press. She accuses Batcham of succumbing to the lies told by Indians. He and his ilk are responsible for encouraging disaffection and sedition. They embarrass the Government of India by her Majesty's loyal opposition. Duncan is very touchy about the criticism of the British administration. She believes that the British in India could do no wrong. This is not a 'balanced' approach, for which she has been praised because of the portrayal of a balanced picture of Elgin society in *The Imperialist*. Her vision, however, gets distorted in India. All those who criticize the Anglo-Indian administration become the butt of Duncan's attack, be they the British numbers of Parliament or the Indian patriots. It can thus be argued that like George Browne, Duncan too believed that India belonged to the Anglo-Indians. The novel ends on a note of pathos. One can discern a sense of longing mixed with the note of pathos. India is referred to by some as a land of regrets. The narrator, however, comments: "The regrets are felt exclusively by those who are going.

The satisfactions of retirement are obscure, and the project of devoting a shrunken end of existence to the solicitous avoidance of bronchitis is not inviting." (306) Doesn't the lament of suffering and sacrifice appear in the end, hollow? And all the talk of the whiteman's burden in reality, turns out to be the white man's privilege of lording over the Indians, which he is loath to give up. Hence the regrets which make the ending of the novel ambivalent.

Vernon's Aunt[8] is an inane book, which McKenna terms as an "example of lack of taste on Duncan's part, an error that must have embarrassed her deeply; considering her convictions about the necessity for discrimination." (149) It appeared serially for *Idler* before being published in a book form. The British were ignorant yet curious about exotic India, always willing to lap up anything that would enlighten them about India. Duncan took this opportunity to open a window of India for the British to see all the colour and darkness that was India, and make some money in the process. It is Duncan's first attempt to avoid the personal voice in which she had spoken in the previous books. Mrs. MacIntyre in *The Memsahib*, though a third person narrator, is, in fact, Duncan herself. Duncan wrote mostly from personal experience. Her characters are also usually based on some real person. In this book, however, she chose a character, a middle-aged unmarried woman, who was far removed from her own person. Here she attempts to present a world in which manners are more important than the men and women who practise them.

Vernon's Aunt is another travelogue, fourth in a series, which details the Indian experiences of Lavinia Moffat, as she goes through unfamiliar terrain and faces impossible situations, some naturally funny, others ridiculous and exaggerated. Miss Moffat's nephew, Vernon Hawkins, lives in India. Like a typical colonial, she decides to pay a visit to India to find out to "what extent the natives actually were adopting our civilization, our clothes and the Thirty Nine Articles." (2)

To make her Indian adventure mere interesting she decides to give her nephew a surprise by arriving unannounced. On her arrival in Bombay, an impossible situation develops. She is received by a person whom she mistakes to be her nephew, and for fifteen pages a stupid charade is played between the two. When at last it is revealed that the young man had mistaken Miss Moffat to be his wife who had lost her memory. The whole affair is too melodramatic to be credible. On her train journey she meets all sorts of people but none is able to satisfy her curiosity about India. She remarks cryptically: "Nothing is more annoying in India than the persistence with which people lament their fate in living there, and shut their eyes to the blessing, not to say the luxuries they enjoy." (62)

Her nephew lives in a forest, where she is taken on an elephant. She has come out to "gather up remarkable experiences" (112) in the quaint Orient. Living in a tent in the middle of a forest, surrounded by wild beasts, an elephant ride, a tiger who turns out to be a cat, and the misadventure with Mr. Bux, Miss Moffat has basketful of experiences of her journey from civilization to savagery.

The novel is one in a string of works by Anglo-Indian writers who dwell upon the difference between the two societies—the difference in language, customs, tradition, outlook and attitude. It also shows there is hardly any communication between the two societies; the British remain aloof and refuse to mingle with Indians. Ms. Moffat is surprised when she notices that "Vernon himself had not Orientalized in the slightest degree. He was even more British than when he left home." (167) This lack of communication between the two communities resulted in mutual suspicion and ultimately in the alienation of the British. The plot of the novel is contrived and implausible which reveals one of her major failings as a novelist: her inability to weave plot and character together. The inevitable snake—a python in the case—centipedes and other such creatures also make an appearance to complete the circus show that was India. Such various stuff might make a good journalistic copy, it fails as a novel.

The Story of Sonny Sahib (1894) is Duncan's only work which is directly linked with the events of the Mutiny of 1857. The idea was perhaps suggested by an old ayah, who had been through the Mutiny and remembered the sad times. The novel deals with the well established theme of superiority of the English blood.

The novel begins during the Mutiny. Sonny Sahib is a little white infant, who is saved by his Indian ayah, when his father is away and his mother is critically ill. During the evacuation of Cawnpore, Tooni, the ayah, is informed that the English convoy will be attacked. Sure that Sonny's mother would anyway die, she escapes with the child, takes him to her homeland, and thus saves his life. He grows up at her house, without being aware of his true identity, but later events prove the superiority of his race and blood. Duncan's depiction of the Mutiny is one-sided as the emphasis is focused on the cruelty of Indian sepoys and treachery of Nana sahib. It was customary in Anglo-Indian writing to paint the Indians, especially the Indian nationalists as blackguards and villains. Writing abort forty years after the event. Duncan describes some of the gory details with perfect composure—even with a bit of grim irony. The boy has to be different, but in a superior way, and Duncan gives several examples to establish Sonny's superiority. The blue eyes and white skin of Sonny Sahib mark him as different though he learned the language of the "little brown boys." (20) He was sharp in his bargain, always got more for his money and "invariably divided his purchase with whoever happened to be his bosom friend at the time . . . in which he differed altogether from the other boys and which made it fair perhaps." (21) The boy is white, better and fair—these are explicitly racial propositions. When Sonny Sahib was six years old, "He wanted to pretend. It was his birthright to pretend." (21) But the other boys were not interested in play-acting. Only Sunny had imagination, the native boys lacked this quality. He had more of the spirit of adventure, as "he was the only boy in Rubbulgarh who cared to climb a tree that had no fruit on it, or would venture beyond the lower branches even for mangoes or tamarinds." (22) Thus, Sonny Sahib's superiority is established beyond a doubt. Duncan doesn't miss the opportunity to inform her young readers that "perhaps nobody has told you why the English are called Sahibs in India. It is because they rule there." (41) A sense of snug satisfaction is evident.

The tide of fortune turns as Sonny is called by the Maharajah of Chita to act as a companion of the young prince where, even in the face of a threat to life, Sonny refuses to divulge, as a matter of honour, the maharajah's military secret to British troops, thus establishing his stout English character, a fact Col. Starr can't help reminding the Maharajah at the end of the novel: "Your highness will remember," said the English soldier for the pleasure of saying it, "he did not tell." However, the Maharajah, being an Indian, is unable to appreciate this gesture and wonders "He is not of our blood, why should he have kept silence?" The Canadian Duncan, thus, establishes the British superiority over the Indians.

The four novels discussed above form a group. In these early Anglo-Indian works Duncan explores, with curiosity and enthusiasm the Anglo-Indian world—their life, their hopes and despairs.

NOTES

1. Misao Dean, "Canadian Nationality in Sara Jeannette Duncan's international Novels, M.A. Dissertation, Carleton University, Ottawa, 1982. Microfiche.
2. Edward Said, *Orientalism* (London: Routledge and Kegan Paul, 1978).
3. Benita Parry, *Delusions and Discoveries: Studies on India in the British Imagination 1880-1930* (New Delhi: Orient Longman, 1972).
4. Sara Jeannette Duncan, *The Simple Adventures of a Memsahib* (New York: Appleton, 1893).
5. G.B. Burgin, "A Chat with Sara Jeannette Duncan," *The Idler*, VIII (August 1895).
6. Frank Birbalsingh, "Sara Jeannette Duncan's Indian Fiction," *World Literature Written in English*, 16, 1 (April 1977).
7. Dennis Kincaid, *The British Social Life in India 1608-1937* (London: Routledge and Kegan Paul, 1973).
8. Sara Jeannette Duncan, *Vernon's Aunt* (London: Chatto and Windus, 1894).

Connecting Worlds: A Study of Arun Mukherjee's *Postcolonialism: My Living*

VIJAY SHESHADRI
University of Mysore

The space of an émigré writer in the creative world is a quizzical one. Culturally transplanted, a Can-Asian writer attempts to map the culture from which s/he hails living in an alien culture space through the naturalized language, English.

A Can-Asian writer uses his self/exile, space and time to chisel an art that would embody his real as well as imagined experience. To her or him, reality is an artifact and it exits only if it is made. Like any artifact, the production can be good or bad. Due to two geographical and culture space, the South Asian writer's 'dissemination' is due to perpetual inhabitation on the murky, shifting boundaries. Evidently, this provides him or her the advantageous perspective to resist all notions of centrality, whether it be the imperial centre or the newly configured national centre/grid. Hence, decentering, pluralism, marginality and hybridity characterize South Asian writings. The very act of writing in this case constitutes an act of exploration, interrogation, an acquisition of a voice, which inevitably diminishes the alienness of the "othered" leading to a neo-cultural configuration..

If one focuses on the writings of Arnold Itwaru, Arun Mukherjee, Anita Rau Badami, Himani Banerjee, Lakshmi Gill, Uma Parameswaran, Jamili Ismail and Aruna Srivastava, one can see that their works pave way for the reconstruction of a nation and notion, entailing variegated dimensions such as socio-cultural, geo-politico-historical investigations.

Reading them will also help one to locate some of the commonalties these writers represent for better understanding of the way cross-culturalism, multiculturalism works and operates. Indeed, it could lead to questions such as, can Can-Asian writers index themselves the same way as Canadian born writers do? If not why and how? Is it possible to view Can-Asian writings as an expression against the mainstream Canadian representation, a way of re-vision and sub-version? Or is it an attempt to challenge the orthodox view of a "National" Literature? Has South Asian writing made an impact on conception of nation-state or reinforced alternative expressions of nation in Canada much as Quebec and the first world? Are Can-Asians ghettoized? If so, how and why? Has Can-Asia lucubrations influenced the publishing industry, Television and print media and so forth?

Postcolonialism: My Living by Arun Mukherjee debates the labeling of literatures of the non-first world as postcolonial literature. The book is a conglomeration of essays and seminar papers, classroom debates, cartographing Arun Mukherjee's career as an academic teaching Postcolonial Literature in a Canadian university. Divided into five sections, the book postmortems Postcolonialism vis-à-vis concept, nation, gender, reading and theorizing.

Interrogating Postcolonialism, "the first section of the book at the outset explains what is Postcolonial literature in the first world academic institutions especially Canada. In Arun Mukherjee's words: "A typical course in Postcolonial Literature 'covers' five regions: Australia-New Zealand, Canada, the Caribbean, Africa and South Asia."[1] It is quite evident here that what used to be taught as Commonwealth Literature earlier now figures under the rubric of Postcolonial literature. Moreover all these five regions are clubbed because they share the "common experience" of Colonialism. Moreover, it is quite obvious that Canadian Academic is ushering in a theoretical framework that is absolutely marked by homogeneity, which has no mooring in reality. Arun Mukherjee is at pains to note that such labeling as Postcolonial Literature reduces the rich diversity to a literature of resistance, an angst due to erasure of precolonial identity and language.

Debating the approach of Bill Ashcroft and Helen Tiffin et al in *The Empire Writes Back*, especially on the subtitle, "Theory and Practice in Postcolonial Literatures,"[2] for completely neglecting the issues of class, caste, race and gender in adjudicating the literatures from the non-first world, Arun Mukherjee observes: "Acknowledgement of differences would force us to admit that the impact of colonialism is only one element in the history of societies which go back thousands of years. It would force us to admit that, besides the inequalities produced by colonialism, there are other, older inequalities of race, caste, class and gender which must be taken into account in our reading of literatures from these societies. We might then come to realize that teaching of these five "regions" by the means of three or four selected texts from each "region" is a very arbitrary arrangement and that, in order to do justice to the literatures of these societies, separate courses on them need to be taught." (6)

Arun Mukherjee points out that postcolonial literature is taught in the Canadian universities only in terms of "writing back" and not in terms of what Dionne Brand, the Caribbean Canadian writer avers: "I do not write back to anyone but 'write home.' As a teacher of such literatures, Arun Mukherjee consciously remarks the lacuna in framing such a syllabi marked by pedagogical problems: "Until these material conditions are brought to light, until their contradictions and their detrimental effects are acknowledged, the teaching and theorizing of their world literatures remain yet another gesture of objectification of their world cultures and societies, despite these theorists' claims of radicalism". (15)

He condemns the branding of postcolonial writing by Ashcroft and Helen Tiffin as "three important features of all postcolonial writing. The silencing and marginalizing of the postcolonial voice by the imperial centre; the abrogation of this imperial centre within the text; and the active appropriation of the language and culture of that centre". (Ashcroft et al 83)

The assessment of Ashcroft and Helen Tiffin, it is quite apparent, exhibits sweeping generalizations, discrimination and is exclusionist. Arun Mukerjee is disturbed to note the ignorance of the supporters of Postcolonial literature at not noting the internal hierarchies within a nation. She draws our attention to M.R. Anand's *Untouchable*, the emergence of dalit writing like Barbara

Joshi's anthology *Untouchable: Voices from the Dalit Liberation Movement* (1986), Kancha Ilaiah's *Why I am not a Hindu*, Omprakash Valmiki's *Jhoothan*, and Mohan Dass Naimishray's *Apane Apane Pinjare*. The non-inclusion of such writing which is Indian language literature that exhibits repositories of Indianness as opposed to Indian English literature which is elitist and "Anglicized", Mukherjee feels that Postcolonialism's eclecticism does not genuinely capture to give a holistic picture of the nations from which the books originate.

In the chapter "How Shall We Read South Asian Canadian Texts?" Arun Mukherjee tells us how South Asian Texts are bracketed as Canadian and non-Canadian. The pressure of having an exclusive Canadian element/component either in journals or a novel, tellingly appears in the changes of appellation of *The Toronto South Asian Review* started by M. G. Vassanji in 1982 to *The Toronto Review of Contemporary Writing Abroad* in 1993. M.G. Vassanji's comment, which is perhaps pessimistic, is apt here: "I have never sensed any passion behind that label "South Asian"—no political front, not even a loosely defined conscious aesthetic or the probing for one: it seemed to be simply a very convenient and the least discomfiting umbrella to fit under. No controversies, no eloquent voices raised, as happened in the black or Afro-communities. No real anger, but certainly resentment. Docility? Perhaps "South Asians" feel close enough to the mainstream to feel that goal achievable—and so everyone for himself, scrambling to get out of the hole and into the sun of recognition." (6)

This, in fact, is a typical instance of acquired behaviour superseding instinctual behaviour, exhibiting Darwinian trait of survival of the fittest! Similarly, Frank Davey's attribution of a footnote to Nino Ricci, M.G. Vassanji and Rohinton Mistry in his *Post-National Arguments: The Politics of the Anglophone Canadian Novel since 1967,* is viewed by Arun Mukherjee in these candid words: "If one of the foremost Canadian critics does not know how to make a sense of these novels in Canadian context, it would be futile to expect anything from those who review for newspapers and journals." (35)

Let me repeat the response of the *Toronto Star* and Phoebe-Lou Adam of the *Atlantic Monthly* to South Asian writing in Canada, especially on Mistry's *A Fine Balance,* to highlight the accommodation of texts by the Canadian universities with a priori, in order to suit their ideological framework: "The local colour frequently turns repulsive. The Bombay of this novel is a city where sewers are in disrepair, where street food vendors practice doubtful hygiene, and where the wall of Gustad's apartment building . . . is used as a public toilet. The most disgusting, and macabre, imagery involves according to traditional practice" (1991, K 13, *Toronto Star*) "Mr. Mistry's novel . . . includes such acid comments on Indian politics, metropolitan services, sanitation and the corruption of Indira Gandhi's government that one can readily see why the author now lives in Toronto." (124, *The Atlantic Monthly*)

The second section, "Postcolonialism in Canada," begins with the problem of defining a Nation and the politics involved in the shaping and construction of a nation. The Canada that is hoisted as a Nation to the outside world is a white middle-class Canadian experience, an admixture of Whiteness and Candianness. In the words of Dionne Brand: "Culture is organized around Whiteness through various 'para-statal bodies including the CBC, The National Film Board, the Canada Council and other provincial and metropolitan councils and through private media and cultural and educational institutions." (78)

In this process of making a national definition, the non-white peoples are left out. Dionne Brand's comments are apt here again: "When I come back to Toronto from the Playas del Este, I will pass a flashing neon sign hanging over the Gardiner Express Way. 'Lloyds Bank' it will say. Lloyds, as in Lloyds of London. They got their bullshit start insuring slave cargo."[4]

It is in Arun Mukherjee's classroom space where the students, text, teacher interface occurs, the most telling issues related to Postcolonialism emerge. She is at her best here when she comments: "I cannot forget an exchange that occurred in one of my classes while studying Vassanji's *No New Land.* A South Asian student addressed a group of White Canadian students and said: "I am glad that this text will make you do the kind of work I have to do when I read the western texts and have to learn about all those allusions by doing some legwork." (82)

Similarly, the introduction of a course on Aboriginal writers and writers of colour in Canada by Arun Mukherjeeprompts a journey of Discovery of Canada. Her comments are apropos to the situation: "My white students say that the course offers them an insight into the cultural and historical realities of their non-white friends' background. My non-white students, on the other hand, find the course content appealing because it validates them by representing their lives. They say that this is the only course where they read books that have something to do with their lives." (85)

It is quite clear here that texts by the non-whites become the 'context zone,' prompting a culture of appreciation, enabling the reader to read other words and their sensibilities that are outside the purview of his or her immediate cultural context. In other words, such an attempt eschews one of becoming a *koopa manduka* or frog in the well. As a teacher of such texts, Arun Mukherjee insists that at times she is cultural outsider teaching texts that are not written by Indians, while teaching Indian texts she becomes a cultural insider. Hence, labeling of such texts by non-whites as not Canadian Arun Mukherjee feels is as good a comment passed by a school superintendent in Arkansas refusing to have foreign languages taught at secondary level: "If English was good enough for Jesus, it's good enough for you."[5] A typical instance of colonized becoming the colonizer!

"Postcolonialism and Gender" is an interesting section highlight the "Othering" of non-first world and non-white women writers by white woman. Using Charlotte Perkins Gilman's *Herland*, a recovered feminist classics of 1915 as an exemplar, Arun Mukherjee comments: "I began reading the text with great enthusiasm. But half way into it I recoiled in horror since it seemed to wipe out all the non-white women in order to create the racially pure utopia of *Herland.* Hadn't my senior colleague, I wondered, noticed this textural genocide?" (110)

The women in canonical texts are invariably paradigms of the white women. For instance, Claire Harris is called an immigrant writer; Prairie writer Margaret Atwood is a Canadian writer. Similarly, writing by Aboriginal and Racial minority is dubbed as Maritime writing, West Coast writing, Prairie writing etc. Bharati Mukherjee could not be a Canadian writer since she "didn't grow up playing in snow."[6] Incidentally, Gilbert and Gubar's *No Man's Land* (1988) and *Norton Anthology of Literature by Women* sidelines non-white women by making just tangential references. Frank Lentricchia's observation on Gilbert and Gubar seems apt here. He calls them "authors of manichean sexual allegory."[7] Such attitudes of white women are deftly dealt by Arun Mukherjee in the following words: "I am suggesting, then, that feminist literary theory has become a totalizing, a universalizing discourse, very much like the androcentric theory it had revolted against." (128) Thus feminist approaches of the white women are a boon for forces that usher in postindustrial societies and hence a neo-imperialist world order in making.

Section VI, "Reading the Texts" adds on a new dimension to texts hitherto being studied for a fairly long period like Mulk Raj Anand's *Untouchable*, Anita Desai's *Clean Light of the Day*, Bessie Head's *Dialogue with India*, to mention a few. Arun Mukherjee exhales fresh breath into these texts with her rich experience of two diverse contrasting cultural contexts—Canada and India.

"Capital-T Theory", the last section provides insights into concepts like universals, Postmodernism and Postcolonialism. Tracking the history of the term 'Universal" from Aristotle's time through Dr. Johnson to the present, Arun Mukherjee takes recourse to critically examine the politics operating on the term Universal, quoting the responses of the likes of Wole Soyinka, Chinua Achebe, Dionne Brand, Arnold Rampersad, Tzevetan Todorov, Edward Said to explore the term Universal in its myriad manifestations. The comments of Soyinka, Achebe, Todorov and Said are pertinent here: Wole Soyinka views 'Universal Men' as a 'Universal humanoid abstraction' while Achebe suggests that the word 'Universal' is nothing more than a 'synonym' for the narrow, self-serving parochialism of Europe.[8] Todorov and Said opine that the word universal has so far been used in an ethnocentric fashion: "The so-called universality of many theoreticians of the past and present as nothing more nor less than unconscious ethnocentrism, the projection of their own characteristic on a grand scale. What has been presented as universality has in fact been a fair description of white males in a few western European countries. This failure however should not lead us to abandon the idea itself for such an abandonment would lead us to renounce the very idea of shared humanity, and this would be even more dangerous then ethnocentric universalism."[9]

Similarly, the word 'Universal' assumes a different dimension in Feminist discourses, especially by the white appealing as an essentialist term arguing that women all the world over are same. Elizabeth Spelman's comments are apt in this connection: "if there is an essential womanness that all women have and have always had, then we needn't know anything about any women in particular. . . . If all women have the same story 'as women,' we don't need a chorus of voices to tell the story."[10]

Through thought-provoking captions like Whose Postmodernism? And Whose Postcolonialism?, Arun Mukherjee critiques the way Postmodernists and Postcolonialists view texts by non-whites from the Eurocentric cultural prerogatives. Arun Mukherjee's comments highlight these prerogatives: "Postmodernism is not an innocent term, a mere label to designate a cultural phenomenon, for those who have been through the experiences of colonialism. Because of our societies, the so-called third world, have been denigrated as 'backward' by those who consider themselves 'modern.'" (216)

Again, "Postcolonial theory constructs its centre-periphery discourse, it also obliterates the fact that postcolonial societies also have their own internal centres and peripheries, their own dominants and marginals. It creates the Bakhtinian "heteroglossia" of literary and social discourse in postcolonial societies that arises from conflicts of race, class, gender, language, religion, ethnicity and political affiliation." (222) It is quite apparent here that the non-first world peoples are forced to look at white discourse as the only on-going prominent debate, a debate that erases the individual and cultural identities of the non-whites by consenting to be under the rubric of the western notion of Post-colonialism.

In sum, a work like *Postcolonialism: My Living* alerts one to such discursive issues like Postmodernism and Postcolonialism and eschews one not to suffer from cultural amnesia. It also prompts quashing of boundaries between literature, to view literature as a holistic entity, in the process paving way for change in attitudes and minds, while acknowledging the literatures of the world better understanding, fellowship and betterment of humanity. Texts like *Postcolonialism: My Living* provide the context for appreciating the emergent New Literatures and prompt a "culture of appreciation" to be developed and realized. Perhaps that should be the first and cardinal task, since we are dwelling in a world of flux.

NOTES

1. Arun Mukherjee, *Postcolonialism: My Living* (Toronto: TSAR, 1998), p. 4.
2. Bill Ashcroft et al, *The Empire Writes Back: Theory and Practice in Postcolonial Literatures* (London: Routledge, 1983), p. 83.
3. Dionne Brand, *Chronicles of the Hostile Sun* (Toronto: William-Wallace, 1984), p. 78.
4. "Bread out of Stone," *Language in Her Eye: View on Writing and Gender by Canadian Women Writing in English,* ed. Libby Scheier et al (1990), p. 52.
5. John Edwards, *Multilingualism* (London: Penguin, 1995), p. 204.
6. Uma Parameswaran, "Ganga in Assiniboine" *A Meeting of Streams: South Asian Canadian Literature*, ed. M.G. Vassanji (Tornoto: TSAR, 1985), p. 86.
7. Frank Lentricchia, "Andiamo," *Critical Inquiry*, 14, 2 (winter).
8. Chinua Achebe, *Hopes and Impediments: Selected Essays (1965-1987)* (London: Heinemann, 1988), p. 52.
9. Tzvetan Todorov, "Race, Writing and Culture." *Race, writing and Difference*, ed. Henry Louis Gates (Chicago: The University of Chicago Press, 1988), p. 374.
10. V. Elizabeth Spelman, *Inessential Woman: Problems of Exclusion in Feminist Thought.* (Boston: Beacon Press, 1988), p. 159.